YALE UNIVERSITY
**Mrs. Hepsa Ely Silliman
Memorial Lectures**

# DISCARD

# SEARCHING

# BETWEEN

# THE

# STARS

## LYMAN
## SPITZER, JR.

NEW HAVEN AND
LONDON
YALE
UNIVERSITY
PRESS

Published with assistance from the foundation
established in memory of Phillip Hamilton McMillan
of the Class of 1894, Yale College.

Figure 1.2 is a photograph of NGC 205 and is reproduced by permission of the Palomar Observatory, California Institute of Technology. Figure 1.3 is a photograph of NGC 3031 and is reproduced by permission of the Palomar Observatory, California Institute of Technology. Figure 1.5 is a photograph obtained with the University of Michigan Curtis-Schmidt telescope at the Cerro Tololo Interamerican Observatory. Figure 2.2 is adapted from observations by G. Westerhout and is used by permission of F. J. Kerr and P. D. Jackson. Figure 2.3 is adapted from Dickey, Salpeter, and Terzian, *Astrophysical Journal Supplements* 36: 93 (1978). Figure 2.4 is a photograph obtained with the 48-inch Schmidt telescope, Palomar Observatory, California Institute of Technology. Figure 2.5 is adapted from Hobbs, *Astrophysical Journal* 157: 149 (1969). Figure 3.2 is adapted from Rogerson, Spitzer, Drake, Dressler, Jenkins, Morton, and York, *Astrophysical Journal* (Letters) 181: L98 (1973). Figure 3.3 is a photograph from the National Aeronautics and Space Administration. Figure 3.4 is a drawing from the National Aeronautics and Space Administration. Figure 3.5 is adapted from Rogerson, Spitzer, Drake, Dressler, Jenkins, Morton, and York, *Astrophysical Journal* (Letters) 181: L98 (1973). Figure 4.4 is adapted from Savage and Mathis, *Annual Review of Astronomy and Astrophysics* 17: 86 (1979). Figure 4.5 is adapted from Rogerson and York, *Astrophysical Journal* 186: L95 (1973). Figure 5.1 is adapted from Spitzer and Jenkins, *Annual Review of Astronomy and Astrophysics* 13: 134 (1975). Figure 5.2 is adapted from Federman, Glassgold, and Kwan, *Astrophysical Journal* 227: 471 (1979). Figure 5.3 is adapted from Spitzer, Cochran, and Hirshfeld, *Astrophysical Journal Supplements* 28: 383 (1974). Figure 6.1 is adapted from York, *Astrophysical Journal* (Letters) 193: L127 (1974). Figure 6.2 is adapted from Snow, Weiler, and Oegerle, *Astrophysical Journal* 234: 510 (1979). Figure 7.3 is adapted from McKee and Ostriker, *Astrophysical Journal* 218: 159 (1977). Figure 7.4 is adapted from Kutner, Tucker, Chin, and Thaddeus, *Astrophysical Journal* 215: 526 (1977). Figure 7.5 is adapted from Thaddeus, *Star Formation*, IAU Symposium No. 75 (1977), p. 50

"Fire and Ice" is from *The Poetry of Robert Frost*, edited by Edward Connery Lathem. Copyright 1923, © 1969 by Holt, Rinehart and Winston. Copyright 1951 by Robert Frost. Reprinted by permission of Holt, Rinehart and Winston, Publishers.

Designed by James J. Johnson
and set in Melior type.
Printed in the United States of America by
Vail-Ballou Press, Binghamton, N.Y.

*Library of Congress Cataloging in Publication Data*

Spitzer, Lyman, Jr., 1914–

Searching between the stars.

(Mrs. Hepsa Ely Silliman memorial lectures; 46)
Bibliography: p.
Includes index.
1. Interstellar matter.   2. Astronautics in astronomy. I. Title. II. Series.
QB790.S68        523.1'12        81–13138
ISBN 0–300–02709–5        AACR2

10  9  8  7  6  5  4  3  2  1

# The Silliman Foundation Lectures

On the foundation established in memory of Mrs. Hepsa Ely Silliman, the President and Fellows of Yale University present an annual course of lectures designed to illustrate the presence and providence of God as manifested in the natural and moral world. It was the belief of the testator that any orderly presentation of the facts of nature or history contributed to this end more effectively than dogmatic or polemical theology, which should therefore be excluded from the scope of the lectures. The subjects are selected rather from the domains of natural science and history, giving special prominence to astronomy, chemistry, geology, and anatomy. The present work constitutes the forty-sixth volume published on this foundation.

To my family

# Contents

# List of Figures

# Preface

Giving the Silliman Lectures in 1978 afforded me a welcome opportunity to review our extensive results on interstellar matter, obtained with the Copernicus satellite since its launch six years earlier. The present book follows the Lectures in describing the Copernicus effort as part of a broad program of research on the interstellar medium. Primary emphasis is placed on information obtained during the decade 1970–80, including not only the Copernicus data, but also microwave observations from radio telescopes on the ground and some X-ray results of particular relevance for interstellar studies.

Preparation of the Princeton telescope-spectrometer for Copernicus and analysis of the observations obtained have taken much of my research time for two decades. My interest in the general theory of interstellar matter extends over an even longer period. The results obtained in all this research seem to me both fascinating and important, and I have a natural interest in presenting them to a wide audience. Hence a major goal in writing this book has been to interest nonspecialists as well as specialists.

To reach those who are not specialists in science, the use of mathematics has been minimized. Numbers have been used in illustrations of principles and in the comparison of theory with observation, but, with very few exceptions, equations have been neither derived nor applied in the main text. Some familiarity with stars, atoms, and light waves has been assumed, but for those whose exposure to physics is not detailed or recent, brief reviews of physical principles have been included where relevant. Simple analogies have been used wherever possible, and brief summaries have been provided for all chapters after the first. College students who have some background in physics or laymen who have pursued astronomy as a hobby may enjoy following here the detailed chain of observation and theory that advances science. For those who wish a more general overview, chapters 1, 3, and 7 may be of particular interest.

The scientific specialist who is familiar with physical principles but not with the details of astronomical research may enjoy this book as a brief and readable survey of a central research field. Although the presentation is simple, an attempt has been made to give all the essential steps in each chain of scientific reasoning. Material which is of interest to readers with a sophisticated scientific background but is not needed for understanding the main text is occasionally presented in parentheses. Thus, several brief explanations of interesting, but somewhat peripheral, scientific topics are treated in this manner, as are a number of simple equations; for those familiar with mathematics, an equation can be more readily understood than the same idea expressed in words. The discussion in chapter 7 on fitting the complicated real world with deliberately simplified theoretical models may interest scientific specialists as well as nonspecialists.

To achieve brevity, many fascinating topics in interstellar research have been omitted. I particularly regret that there is virtually no discussion of research with either infrared or long radio wavelengths.

The scientific research discussed here must be regarded as work in progress rather than as a completed structure. We cannot claim any detailed understanding of the cosmic cycle, starting with the explosion of a supernova and leading to mixing of heavy elements with hydrogen and helium, formation of dust particles and clouds of cool gas, and finally the condensation of the gas into new stars and stellar systems, which produce supernovae anew. But our knowledge of these topics has increased significantly in the last decade. I hope that the reader will share the excitement of penetrating Nature's veil, of finding rational, self-consistent explanations for complex phenomena extending over many light years of space, and of approaching some concept of how our Galaxy evolves through aeons of time.

Although I have mentioned the names of a very few astronomers who pioneered in earlier work, no names have been given in connection with results achieved after 1970. All this research has been the product of many scientists working sometimes separately, sometimes together. The list of references at the end gives a few of the names associated with this research, but to give credit fairly to all the creative and imaginative scientists engaged in these exciting fields would be impossible in this brief, nontechnical summary. Let me record here my indebtedness at least to other members of the Copernicus group, whose names appeared in the May 1973 publication of our first results: J. F. Drake, K. Dressler, E. B. Jenkins, D. C. Morton, J. B. Rogerson, and D. G. York. In his capacity as Executive Director of our Copernicus program until launch (co-Principal Investigator since that time), Jack Rogerson's insight, imaginative approach to novel problems, and overall sound judgement were indispensable to the success of this enterprise. Like essentially all U.S. space astronomy, the *Copernicus* project has been fully supported by the U.S. National Aeronautics and Space Administration.

It is a pleasure to acknowledge the assistance received during the preparation of this book. During the spring term of 1980, when I wrote the manuscript, I was a visitor at the Institut d'Astrophysique in Paris, at the invitation of the Director, Dr. Jean Audouze, to whom I am greatly indebted for warm and generous hospitality. Helpful and much appreciated comments on this material were received from my scientific colleagues, especially those at Princeton, as well as from members of my immediate family. I am particularly grateful to Dr. Harry L. Shipman at the University of Delaware and to my daughter, Dionis S. Griffin, for very detailed suggestions, which were central in a thoroughgoing revision of the entire manuscript.

*Princeton University Observatory*
*March 1, 1981*

# 1

# The Cosmic Cycle of Birth and Death

The Universe is mostly empty space. The total volume occupied by the stars is only a very tiny fraction of the volume between them. As an example, we take the space between our own star, the Sun, and the closest neighboring star. Although a light ray takes only two seconds to travel a distance equal to the radius of the Sun, four years are required for light from the Sun to reach the nearest star, which is said to be at a distance of four light years. The ratio of these two times is about $6 \times 10^7$, or 60,000,000. The sphere of radius four light years centered at the Sun has a volume of space that is greater than the Sun's by the cube of $6 \times 10^7$, which is about $2 \times 10^{23}$. Except for the Sun at the center, this sphere seems very nearly empty.

But not quite. A very slight trace of gas is present throughout its volume. This gas is mainly hydrogen, the lightest known element. If an ordinary cup (with a volume of about 200 cm³) were placed a light year or two away from the Sun, the number of hydrogen atoms found in it would be about 20 on the average (along with about 2 helium atoms). By comparison, the number of oxygen and nitrogen atoms in such a cup in the normal air around us would be enormously greater, about $10^{22}$. With each breath of air, we take in about this many atoms—so very many that included among them will be several of the very same atoms inhaled in one breath by Alexander the Great, for example (or by anyone else whose breath was exhaled long enough ago to be thoroughly mixed with the atmosphere all over the Earth).

Although the density of the gas between the Sun and the nearest star is extremely low, the total volume of gas within the sphere centered at the Sun and just reaching to the nearest star is extremely large. As a result, the total mass of hydrogen in this sphere, outside the Sun itself, is equal to a few percent of the Sun's mass. This result is typical of the vast aggregation of stars, or galaxy, in which we live.

1

This disc-shaped system has a thickness of roughly a thousand light years and a diameter about a hundred times greater. In this volume of about $10^{13}$ cubic light years, the mass of the interstellar gas is comparable with the total mass of all the stars in the system! It is no coincidence that the total mass of the stars is comparable with that of the interstellar gas; as pointed out later in this chapter, there is an evolutionary relationship between the gas and the stars.

Outside our own stellar system are other galaxies, at distances ranging all the way from a few hundred thousand to more than ten billion light years away from us. Although some information has been obtained on gas in other galaxies, we shall consider here only the gas within our own system—the Galaxy, as we shall sometimes refer to it. Such emphasis on our own particular surroundings seems unavoidable. Naturally we know much more about our own system, which is close at hand and easily observed in detail, than about other galaxies, in which even the brightest stars appear very faint because of their enormous distances.

So this book concerns the interstellar gas within the Galaxy. In particular, later chapters describe a number of dramatic increases in our understanding of this highly rarified material. These increases, all occurring during the decade 1970–80, were made possible by the new observing tools that became available during this period—principally the *Copernicus* satellite telescope for ultraviolet light and new types of detectors for electromagnetic microwave radiation.

One of the principal reasons for studying the interstellar gas is the significant part played by this material in the evolution of the Galaxy. Stars are formed from interstellar gas; some of these stars die after a few million years and explode, ejecting back into interstellar space much of the hydrogen from which they were formed. More important, such explosions shoot out large amounts of heavier elements, generated by nuclear fusion processes deep in the hot interior of each star. Both the Earth and the Sun have condensed in interstellar space from gas enriched in this way with carbon, oxygen, iron, and other familiar elements within and around us. This cosmic cycle of star birth, death, and explosion, followed by the formation of new stars from the ashes of the old, is described later in this chapter. To understand how this cycle operates, we must know how interstellar gas condenses to form successive generations of new stars. Hence an understanding of star formation is an important goal of interstellar matter studies.

There is another reason for trying to understand what happens in the vast reaches between the stars. Here, as in other research areas, a combination of curiosity and aesthetics motivates many scientists. To find the causes of natural phenomena, to show that many observed events follow from a few simple physical laws—these are challenging objectives. When a theory is successful and ties together different observations in a coherent picture, the personal satisfaction can be great.

These goals have not yet been fully achieved. We do not understand the details of star formation. Indeed, we do not comprehend many of the interstellar phenomena. While we look forward to a fuller understanding, we must realize that each increase in knowledge may open up new fields for us to explore. As in the lines from Tennyson's *Ulysses,*

Yet all experience is an arch wherethro'
Gleams that untravelled world whose margin fades
For ever and for ever when I move.

## THE INITIAL BIG BANG

The cosmic cycle of star birth, death, explosion, and rebirth has not been going on forever. Before discussing the details of this cycle, we ask first: How did it all start? How did the Universe begin? At what stage were the first stars formed? In recent decades, scientists have evolved a theory of the very first stages of this process—the titanic initial explosion of the Universe about fifteen billion $(1.5 \times 10^{10})$ years ago, commonly refered to as the "Big Bang."

According to this theory, the Universe was created as one nearly uniform, fiery gas, expanding at an enormous rate. It may seem presumptuous to apply physical laws as we know them to a primordial event of which we have no direct knowledge. But this is exactly what scientists have done. As we shall see, the results of this theory are in remarkable agreement with the observations, and, as a consequence, the Big Bang hypothesis is now widely accepted.

The nature of the initial explosion is illustrated in figure 1.1, which shows a very small region of the expanding Universe an instant after creation. The straight arrows represent velocities with respect to the material at the center, P, of the figure. At any particular instant after the explosion began, any element of the gas is moving away from any other element with a speed that is in direct proportion to the distance between the two elements. A similar effect occurs with points on the surface of a balloon that is being steadily in-

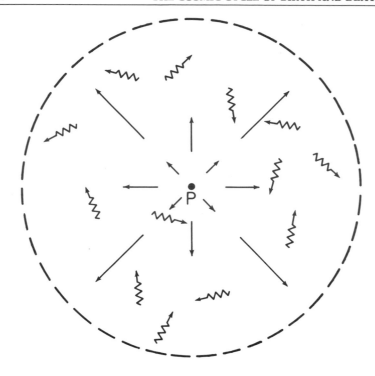

FIGURE 1.1 Expanding material in the Big Bang. A very small fraction of the initial expanding Universe is shown. The straight lines represent velocities of hot gas relative to material at P. The wavy lines represent photons of radiant energy. The dashed circle represents the spherical horizon as seen at P; its radius is the distance travelled by a photon since the moment of creation. Photons produced beyond this horizon cannot reach P until later times.

flated; at any one time the relative velocity of separation of any two points is proportional to the distance between the points.

Whether the Universe as a whole is curved or flat, open or closed, makes no difference at the beginning, since the material at some location P cannot be influenced by anything outside a sphere of radius $c \times t$ centered at P, where $t$ is the time since creation, and $c$ is the velocity of light ($3 \times 10^5$ km sec$^{-1}$). Since no signal can travel faster than light, what has happened outside the sphere at times earlier than $t$ cannot have any effect on events at the location P. Thus the surface of this sphere, represented by a dashed circle in figure 1.1, is as far as a hypothetical observer can see from P at time $t$. This surface is called the horizon. Of course, any actual observer at this stage would vaporize in the twinkling of an eye. It should be emphasized that the location P is arbitrary; the same picture represents any place in the expanding Universe, which, even at this early stage, is enormously larger than the region shown in figure 1.1.

The exploding matter newly created in the Big Bang is assumed to be composed of protons—the nuclei of hydrogen atoms—and neutrons—neutral particles with a mass about equal to the proton mass—together with electrons and other low-mass particles of a more esoteric nature (positrons and neutrinos). The temperature is enormous at first, and the electromagnetic radiation is very intense.

Because the distance to the horizon is so small in early times, the newly created Universe is composed of regions that as yet have no physical connection with each other. At $t = 0.01$ sec, for example, the total mass of neutrons and protons—so-called material particles—inside the local horizon is about equal to the mass of the Earth. The total mass of the Universe that we can see at the present day, out to the most distant galaxies, is greater by a factor of at least $10^{26}$. Thus at $t - 0.01$ sec, the Universe is composed of at least $10^{26}$ expanding units, each of which has only recently made contact with a few surrounding units, and then only at the edges.

The Big Bang theory assumes that the Universe was nearly uniform when it was created. Hence one must believe that more than $10^{26}$ units were created instantaneously, each within its local horizon and with about the same temperature and density. In fact, as we shall see later in this section, present observations imply a rather high degree of uniformity in the early Universe. Thus the theory seems to call for enormous numbers of small bangs (with greater and greater numbers at smaller and smaller $t$), all essentially simultaneous, close together, and nearly identical, but with no physical relationship between them. An aesthetically satisfying theory of creation should involve a simple beginning, but as yet no simple reason has been found why these disconnected regions of the Universe should all be so nearly identical at formation.

If we accept the assumption of nearly complete uniformity initially, it becomes possible to follow theoretically the change in the radiation and the matter as the Universe expands. We trace this evolution here, starting at $t = 0.01$ sec. (At earlier times the particle energies were so great that physicists are not certain as to the phenomena that may have occurred.)

Detailed computations show that at $t = 0.01$ sec, the temperature has the huge value of $10^{11°}$ K. (The K denotes the Kelvin temperature scale—the Centigrade scale shifted so that zero temperature is the so-called *absolute zero*, at $-273°$ Centigrade or $-460°$ Fahrenheit.) At a temperature of $10^{11°}$ K—some ten thousand times hotter than the center of the Sun—the electromagnetic radiation is so intense that its mass density is roughly one hundred million times the correspond-ing mass per unit volume of the protons and neutrons. (According to Einstein, light must have mass, since energy, $E$, is related to mass, $m$, by the familiar equation $E = mc^2$.) Although no place is known in the present Universe where these conditions are now duplicated, all the processes occurring at this early stage of creation seem well under-stood, and established physical theories should be applicable.

As the time increases, different elements of matter rush away from each other, and the temperature falls, much as air in a tank at high pressure cools when the gas is released and expands into the surrounding atmosphere. Some three minutes after creation, the tem-perature has fallen to a cooler $10^{9°}$ K. At this temperature, some neu-trons and protons begin to stick together, without being disrupted immediately by electromagnetic radiation. Each such nuclear fusion reaction between a neutron and a proton will now form a deuteron (denoted by the symbol D)—a particle with the charge of a proton but twice its mass. At room temperature an electron is normally captured in an orbit around a deuteron, forming an atom of deuterium—an *iso-tope* of hydrogen that differs from the normal form by having twice the mass per atom. In the early Big Bang, the deuterium is all ion-ized, with electrons and deuterons moving separately. For $t$ between about 3 and 10 minutes, many deuterons stick together in pairs, or fuse, to form helium nuclei, each with a charge of two protons and a mass equal to that of about four protons.

At greater values of $t$, continuing expansion and decreasing den-sity cause collision rates among deuterons and other light nuclei to fall so low that all such fusion reactions essentially cease. The abun-dance ratios between hydrogen, deuterium, and helium do not change further; the values of these ratios depend on the density of matter—neutrons and protons—during this period of nucleosyn-thesis when the temperature is dropping below $10^{9°}$ K. If the density is relatively high, nuclear reactions will continue a little longer, and more deuterons will stick together to form helium nuclei, reducing the final abundance of deuterium relative to hydrogen or helium. In chapter 4 we shall see how the interstellar abundance of deuterium relative to hydrogen has been measured with the *Copernicus* satellite and has been used in conjunction with the Big Bang theory to deter-mine the density in the Universe.

It is somewhat surprising at first sight that the buildup of elements during the Big Bang stops at helium. This result follows from the instability of the nucleus ($^8$Be) formed from the fusion of two helium nuclei. The formation of carbon and all heavier elements—sometimes called *heavy elements* by astronomers—requires the formation of carbon nuclei by the fusion of three helium nuclei, a process requiring much higher densities than those in the Big Bang during the nuclear fusion phase. (At $t = 3$ min, the material density in the newly created Universe is at most about $10^{-4}$ gm cm$^{-3}$—about a tenth of that in the air around us.) As we shall see later, formation of carbon from helium occurs in due course in stellar cores, where the densities exceed 100 gm cm$^{-3}$.

After the first eventful ten minutes, the expansion of the Universe continues for a long time without any qualitative change. As the distance between any two portions of the gas increases by some factor, the temperature drops by the same factor. The relative velocity of separation between any two portions of the gas also drops with time, since the gravitational self-attraction of the mass present (including radiation, electrons, etc. as well as material particles) decelerates the expansion. The distance, $c \times t$, from each point out to the local horizon increases steadily, of course, as does the amount of material within this local horizon.

Between $10^5$ and $10^6$ years after creation, an important qualitative change occurs. The temperature falls to about 5,000° K, and both hydrogen and helium nuclei start to combine with electrons, forming neutral atoms. A few million years later, the temperature has fallen well below 3,000° K, and the combination of electrons with these positive ions is virtually complete, and most atoms are neutral. The significance of this new phase results from the fact that neutral atoms do not scatter electromagnetic radiation very effectively, in marked contrast to the free electrons that were so numerous earlier. Hence, after ion-electron combination, the radiation streams freely through the gas of hydrogen and helium without affecting it. Matter and radiation are then said to be uncoupled. This uncoupling makes possible the formation of galaxies, the topic of the following section.

We look now at the various ways in which the theory of the Big Bang agrees with the observations. The simplest consequence of the theory is that the galaxies share in the velocities resulting from the initial explosion. Each galaxy recedes from every other galaxy with a velocity directly proportional to the distance between the two. This mutual separation of galaxies produces by the Doppler effect (see p. 30) a shift of the observed spectra to longer wavelengths; this is the well-known "red shift." In 1929 E. P. Hubble pointed out that the observed red shifts of galaxies increased in direct proportion to the distances from us. More recently, this law of Hubble's has been substantiated even for galaxies moving away from us at speeds comparable to that of light. A chief argument for the Big Bang as a theory of creation is that it leads directly to Hubble's law.

Another result of Hubble's law, as explained by the Big Bang theory, is that it gives a definite number for the age of the Universe. If the velocity of separation between two galaxies has remained constant, the time since the separation began is equal to the present distance divided by the velocity. According to Hubble's law, this quotient is the same for all galaxies. There is some uncertainty in the actual distances and also in the extent to which deceleration of the motions has occurred. Best estimates give from 15 to 20 billion (1.5 to $2 \times 10^{10}$) years for the age of the Universe, since the start of the Big Bang. The ages of the oldest stars, as determined from the theory of stellar evolution, are somewhat less, in the range of 10 to 15 billion years. Since the Universe must clearly be somewhat older than the stars in our Galaxy, this agreement is very gratifying.

Another consequence of the Big Bang theory is the existence of electromagnetic radiation. When the temperature is very high during the first few moments, this radiant energy is very intense. Let us examine how the radiation weakens as the Universe expands. According to quantum theory, such radiation is composed of little bundles of wave energy called photons. After uncoupling, photons do not interact with matter and, in consequence, are neither created nor destroyed. Hence, as the Universe expands, the photons become more and more spread out and the number of photons per unit volume decreases in strict proportion to the corresponding number of material particles—protons plus neutrons, including those in atomic nuclei. It so happens that this is true before uncoupling also. Hence the number of photons per material particle remains constant from $t = 0.01$ second onward. As viewed at any point, the photon wavelengths will be shifted by the Doppler effect to greater and greater values as the Universe expands. This universal cosmic radiation field, resulting from the original "fireball" accompanying the Big Bang, is a major prediction of the theory.

This cosmic radiation was first measured in 1965 by A. A. Penzias and R. W. Wilson. A distinguishing feature is that its intensity is so nearly independent of direction. As a radio telescope is pointed toward different directions in the sky, the observed brightness does not vary by more than one part in a thousand. This result indicates that when radiation and matter became uncoupled about $10^6$ years after creation the temperature of the Universe was everywhere constant to about this degree of accuracy.

The present temperature of the cosmic radiation and the present density of matter may be combined to give the material density a few minutes after creation, when nuclear fusion was occurring. Using this density, we can then compute how much hydrogen was converted into helium at this early time. The average photon wavelength in the cosmic radiation is observed to be about 0.2 cm at present, while the number of photons per cubic centimeter is about 500. These numbers correspond to radiation in equilibrium with matter at a temperature of about 3° K. While the average density of matter in the present Universe is less well-known, the best estimates combined with the cosmic radiation measures indicate that there are about $10^9$ times as many photons as protons and neutrons in the Universe. As we have seen, this very large ratio has remained constant throughout the expansion.

The amount of helium produced during the Big Bang in the time interval between 3 and 10 minutes after creation can be computed exactly for this ratio of radiation to matter. The result of this calculation is that one helium atom was produced for every ten atoms of hydrogen, in good agreement with the helium-hydrogen ratio observed in the Sun, the stars, and gas clouds within the Galaxy.

Thus we see that the Big Bang theory brings together in one cohesive picture results obtained in four widely different observational fields. These results are:

1. The observed shift to longer wavelengths of spectra from distant galaxies, with the shift in direct proportion to the distance of each galaxy, in accord with Hubble's law.

2. An age of the Universe, computed from the ratio of galactic distance to velocity, of 15 to 20 billion years, in good agreement with the somewhat lesser ages found for stars.

3. The observed existence of cosmic background radiation, uniform in all directions, corresponding to a temperature of about 3° K.

4. The observed abundance of one helium atom to every ten hydrogen atoms.

This agreement between observation and theory is not sufficiently precise to be conclusive, but it certainly suggests that the Big Bang, as outlined above, really did occur.

## FORMATION OF GALAXIES AND STARS

We have seen that about a million years after creation, the Universe is still a relatively uniform mixture of gas and radiation. There are no stars, no galaxies. Star formation occurs somewhat later, as a result of the self-gravitational attraction of the gaseous material, but only after matter and radiation become uncoupled. A radiation field tends to resist compression, and during the first $10^6$ years, when gas and radiation are firmly coupled together, gravitational condensation is not possible.

The tendency of a gas to condense under its own self-gravitational attraction has been called *gravitational instability*. It was shown by J. H. Jeans more than fifty years ago that this tendency will occur if the amount of mass involved exceeds a certain critical value, now called the *Jeans mass*. According to the theory, the Jeans mass is very large, in general accord with the great masses of stars and stellar systems.

The nature of an instability, and in particular the accelerating rate at which it normally grows, may be illustrated by a very simple example. Consider a needle balanced on its point. In principle, this is a possible equilibrium situation. However, it is easily demonstrated that any tiny departure from equilibrium will grow geometrically—like successive terms in a geometric series; that is, there will be a characteristic time in which this departure, or perturbation, doubles. For a needle balanced on its point, this doubling time is about one-thirtieth of a second. If the upper end of the needle is initially $1 \times 10^{-6}$ cm away from its equilibrium position (which is directly over the tip), then after one doubling time, this distance will increase to $2 \times 10^{-6}$ cm, after two such times to $4 \times 10^{-6}$ cm, then to $8 \times 10^{-6}$ cm, and so on. Evidently in 20 doubling times, corresponding to an increase in the perturbation by a factor of $10^6$, the needle will topple over, even for this very tiny, initial departure from equilibrium. (This rapid growth, which is normal for most types of instability, is referred to as exponential, since the perturbation varies at $10^{at}$, where $a$ is a constant, and $t$ is time.)

For gravitational instability in a Universe which is expanding rather than stationary, this rapid growth does not apply. In this situation, the growth of a perturbation is more nearly linear than geometrical; that is, in each unit of time, a perturbation increases by the addition of roughly the same amount, rather than by multiplication by a constant factor. (More precisely, a density perturbation grows as $t^{2/3}$.) As a result, if the initial perturbations are very small, they may never grow very large. If the expanding gas produced in the Big Bang is to condense into galaxies, and not simply to expand more or less uniformly forever, there must be some nonuniformities in the temperature, density, or velocity right from the initial moment of creation. These need not be large: a change of one part in ten thousand in the overall density from one large region (containing many solar masses of matter) to another will apparently suffice. Indeed, the very high degree of uniformity of the observed cosmic background radiation shows that any initial nonuniformities cannot have been much greater than this small amount. But why did the Universe initially possess nonuniformities of this order? Why should creation have been imperfect in just this way? These are unanswered questions.

Once matter and radiation have become uncoupled, a region in which the gas density slightly exceeds the average value in the Universe at that time can be gravitationally bound. It will expand somewhat further, but its self-gravitational attraction will bring its expansion velocity to a halt, perhaps some $10^7$ to $10^8$ years after creation. It will then start to contract, with an accelerating, inward velocity, perhaps collapsing relatively rapidly toward the end.

Presumably such a condensation becomes transformed into a galaxy or a cluster of galaxies. To follow this development in detail is a complex task, since the final products are themselves rather complicated. Some galaxies are in clusters, some are not. Galaxies also differ dramatically among themselves; some are relatively featureless ellipsoidal systems—so-called elliptical galaxies—with very little interstellar gas (see figure 1.2 which shows a elliptical companion of the great spiral galaxy in the constellation Andromeda) Other galaxies have gaseous discs and develop the spiral arms that are such beautiful characteristics of these systems, which are called spiral galaxies (see figure 1.3, which shows the object listed as No. 81 in the catalog by the eighteenth-century French astronomer, C. Messier). To explain all these complexities requires an intricate theory, which is difficult to verify conclusively when there are no observations of the critical stages, only of the end results.

Hence we pass over the detailed theories of galaxy formation and turn instead to two concepts, or ideas, that are basic to all such theories. The first is the concept of fragmentation, advanced in 1953 by F. Hoyle. Fragmentation occurs under certain conditions, such as constant temperature, which may obtain approximately in an isolated pregalactic cloud of gas. A large mass of gas, somewhat exceeding the Jeans mass, is assumed to be collapsing gravitationally. As it does so, the Jeans mass decreases with increasing density (as $1/\sqrt{\rho}$,

FIGURE 1.2 Elliptical galaxy in the constellation Andromeda. No young stars are present, nor is there any conspicuous interstellar gas and dust. Photograph obtained with the 200-inch Hale telescope.

FIGURE 1.3 Spiral galaxy in the constellation Ursa Major. The spiral arms are regions where hot, young stars are forming continually from interstellar gas. Photograph obtained with the 200-inch Hale telescope.

where $\rho$ is the density), and as a result smaller masses become gravitationally unstable and start to collapse. Thus the collapsing cloud fragments into subclouds, which also start to collapse. In turn, each of these smaller subclouds becomes unstable and fragments into yet smaller units. We can imagine that by a process of successive fragmentation a single collapsing cloud of gas may condense into the enormous number of stars—about $10^{11}$—contained in a typical galaxy.

The second concept relevant to the birth of galaxies concerns the time and location of star formation in a galaxy. It is easier to understand the origin of an elliptical galaxy if we assume that the collapsing gas condenses into stars before the system has reached its final size and shape, and that the system of stars then collapses to the final, featureless state which we now observe. In this state very little gas is left in the system. In spiral galaxies also, some stars may be assumed to originate during the final collapse phase, producing the featureless spheroidal component, devoid of much gas, that is observed in these systems. Such a spheroidal stellar component is evident in the central regions of the spiral galaxy shown in figure 1.3. However, in these spiral systems, unlike elliptical systems, much gas survives the early star-formation phase and forms a rotating disc of interstellar matter; such a *galactic disc* of gas in our own Galaxy provides the focus of this book.

Such a disc is necessarily rather thin. Any motions perpendicular to the disc will soon be much reduced by collisions between different portions of the gas, leaving only the circular motion as the gas revolves about the center of the disc. With no appreciable motions perpendicular to the plane of rotation, the thickness of the disc becomes much smaller than its diameter.

Concentrations of gas within these thin galactic discs continually produce new, highly luminous stars. Such concentrations tend to cluster together in spiral arms and are characterized by absorbing dust particles as well as luminous gas. The hot massive stars born in such spiral arms account for much of the bluish light seen from these arms and produce the spectacular features shown in figure 1.3. At the end of this chapter we shall see how we know that the brightest of these stars were born recently—that is, within the last few million years.

## NUCLEAR BURNING AND ELEMENT FORMATION

The next events we shall consider in the early history of the Universe occur deep inside the newly formed stars. As each star condenses, collapsing under its tremendous self-attraction due to gravity, the innermost layers are steadily compressed. This compression leads to heating, the converse of the cooling produced by the gas expansion during the Big Bang. At the high temperatures produced, the electrons are knocked off the hydrogen and helium nuclei, just as they were during the first million years. At the temperatures exceeding $10^{7}$°K, that are produced at the centers of stars as massive as the Sun, nuclear reactions start afresh, creating heavy elements. The present chemical composition of the solar system, indicated in table 1.1 with respect to the ten most abundant elements, is the result of these nucleogenetic reactions occurring in early generations of stars. We shall now trace the course of these important processes.

This discussion will be restricted to the relatively more massive stars, those that are at least twice as massive as the Sun. The lighter stars do not do much, their central temperatures are low, and their

TABLE 1.1. Properties of Ten Most Abundant Elements

| Element | Symbol | Relative[a] Number | Charge in Atomic Units | Mass in Atomic Units | Number of He Nuclei |
|---------|--------|-------------------|------------------------|----------------------|---------------------|
| Hydrogen | H | 1000. | 1 | 1 | — |
| Helium | He | 100. | 2 | 4 | 1 |
| Carbon | C | 0.4 | 6 | 12 | 3 |
| Nitrogen | N | 0.10 | 7 | 14 | — |
| Oxygen | O | 0.6 | 8 | 16 | 4 |
| Neon | Ne | 0.06 | 10 | 20 | 5 |
| Magnesium | Mg | 0.04 | 12 | 24 | 6 |
| Silicon | Si | 0.04 | 14 | 28 | 7 |
| Sulphur | S | 0.015 | 16 | 32 | 8 |
| Iron | Fe | 0.028 | 26 | 56 | 13[b] |

a. Observed relative numbers of atoms in the Solar System.
b. Four neutrons are also included in this Fe nucleus.

rates of nuclear ractions are so small that during some $1.5 \times 10^{10}$ years—about the age of the present Universe—their production of new elements is relatively small. Furthermore, during this period these lighter stars do not inject much of their mass back into the interstellar medium, so any heavy elements formed would not be returned to the interstellar gas in any case. It is the heaviest stars that have the highest central temperatures and that therefore provide the most efficient ovens for cooking atomic nuclei and generating heavier elements. It is these relatively massive stars, a hundred times as massive as the Sun, in extreme cases, that explode at the end of their lives, injecting heavy elements back into space, where they become part of the next generation of stars.

We turn now to the dominant nuclear process occurring in stars. This is the fusion reaction, in which two nuclei collide and stick together. All nuclei have positive electrical charges, and the mutual repulsive forces between nuclei tend to inhibit the close encounters required for fusion. As a result, two nuclei must be moving toward each other with high velocity for fusion to take place. In a gas at any temperature, all atoms will have random motions, sometimes referred to as thermal motions. At high temperatures, between $10^7$ and $10^{9°}$ K, the thermal velocities of the nuclei are great enough to produce such reactions. Lower temperatures are adequate for reactions between hydrogen nuclei, which have only a single basic unit of charge, but the higher temperatures are needed for collisions between the more highly charged nuclei of carbon and oxygen, with six and eight basic units of positive charge, respectively. When nuclei heavier than protons were forming during the Big Bang, between 3 and 10 minutes after creation, the temperature was well above the minimum required for fusion; it was the drop in density, rather than in temperature, that stopped these reactions. Since the fusion of two nuclei releases energy, and since the reacting elements are destroyed, or at least transformed, this process is often referred to as nuclear burning, even though the process is quite different in detail from the chemical combustion we know.

As the temperature rises inside a contracting, newly formed star, the conversion of hydrogen to helium is the first process of nucleogenesis to occur. When helium was formed during the Big Bang, starting, as we have seen, at about $t = 3$ min, there were many neutrons around, and these stuck to protons to form deuterons, which then fused together to form helium nuclei, each with four units of mass and two of charge. In a star, however, there are usually no free neutrons. (This electrically neutral particle is unstable, decaying into a proton and an electron with a half-life of 11 minutes; thus, after an interval of 11 minutes, half the neutrons present initially will have decayed, and half of the remaining half will have decayed after another 11 minutes, etc.) Because of the absence of neutrons, the formation of helium in a contracting new star must begin with two protons sticking together and ejecting a positron—a positive electron—to form a deuteron. Then the deuterons form helium nuclei, either by sticking together directly, as in the Big Bang, or by adding first one proton and then another. In any case the final result is the conversion of hydrogen into helium, which occurs at temperatures of about $10^{7°}$ K. After a time (about $10^6$ years for the most massive stars), virtually all the hydrogen in the central region of the star will have been converted to helium. Most of the energy radiated by the stars comes from this process of hydrogen fusion, which, in a few decades, may also be available on Earth for the generation of useful power.

Once the hydrogen in the stellar core has been consumed, the core contracts again, increasing the central temperature to about $2 \times 10^{8°}$ K. At this point nuclear burning of the helium begins, with the generation of carbon. As pointed out earlier, two helium nuclei cannot form a stable nucleus. Fusion of helium nuclei involves a three-body process, in which three helium nuclei stick together, forming a carbon nucleus, with a mass and charge equal to 12 and 6 atomic units respectively (see table 1.1).

In this process of carbon formation, it is not necessary for all three helium nuclei to collide with each other simultaneously; two of the nuclei can fuse, forming an unstable nucleus ($^8Be$), which breaks up in a very short time ($2 \times 10^{-16}$sec). If a third helium nucleus collides with the unstable nucleus before the latter decays, there is a good chance that all three particles will stick together permanently, to form a stable carbon nucleus. A high density is required for an appreciable probability of such a collision in so short a time, which is why virtually no carbon or other heavier elements were formed in this way during the Big Bang.

After another interval of many millennia, all the helium in the central region of the massive star will have been converted into carbon and oxygen, in roughly equal amounts. (Sometimes a carbon nucleus will capture another helium nucleus, producing a nucleus of oxygen.) The star continues to contract, with the temperature steadily increasing, and carbon burning begins. In this process two carbon nuclei stick together, with a helium nucleus escaping, leaving a nucleus of neon. By the time that carbon fusion starts, a shell of nearly pure helium is present in the star between the carbon core and the outer primordial layers containing mostly hydrogen. As the star continues to evolve, with the outer envelope expanding to many hundred solar radii, and the core contracting and becoming steadily hotter, the carbon at the center is consumed. Successively heavier elements form at the center of the core, where both the temperature and the density are the greatest. The layered structure of an evolved star with a mass about twenty times that of the Sun is shown in figure 1.4.

This process terminates when a temperature of $5 \times 10^{9°}$ K is reached at the center, at which time the core is composed mostly of iron and its companion elements, chromium and nickel (whose nuclear charges differ by minus or plus two atomic units, or one helium nucleus, respectively, from that of iron). One might wonder why fusion reactions cannot continue in this hot, highly ionized gas, producing nuclei of heavy elements all the way up to uranium. As it happens, the energy released by nuclear fusion decreases rapidly with increasing mass and charge and disappears for iron. Hence the fusion of lighter elements to form iron nuclei releases all the energy available. Production of heavier elements from iron does not release energy but, quite the opposite, requires energy. It is for this reason that a nucleus of one of the very heaviest elements, such as uranium, can release energy by splitting into two nuclei—the nuclear fission process that powers conventional uranium reactors. Hence, when a star has converted the gas at its center into iron, it is literally out of fuel.

What happens? Stars much less massive than the Sun will not die for many more billion of years, but when they finally do meet their

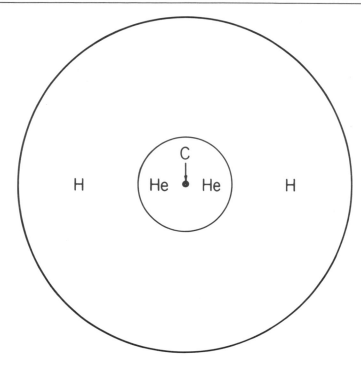

FIGURE 1.4 Structure of an evolved massive star. This diagram shows the layered structure of a massive star, containing about 20 solar masses, shortly before its final explosion. The symbols indicate the dominant elements—hydrogen, helium, and carbon—in each layer. For illustrative purposes, the outer radius of the star has been much decreased; the correct radius is about 200 times greater than that shown. The small inner core, which contains iron and similar elements, is not shown; its outer radius is a small fraction of that for the carbon zone.

end, they will go quietly—they will contract, stop radiating, and grow cold. Stars that are more than about five to ten times as massive as the Sun die a few million years after birth. Their death is spectacular—they explode and for a few weeks emit radiation at a greater rate than all the other stars in a galaxy together, some $10^{11}$ in number. Such an exploding star is called a supernova. The explosion originates at the center and drives a high pressure blast wave out through the surrounding layers of the star, accelerating these regions to velocities of 10,000 km sec$^{-1}$ or more. In the course of the explosion, additional nuclei of iron and its companion elements may be formed. Furthermore, vast quantities of neutrons are produced, and the rapid capture of these neutrons by iron nuclei generates very heavy elements, up to, and even beyond uranium. When the blast wave reaches the surface, the material escapes, scattering carbon, oxygen, lead, and most other elements into interstellar space.

An additional, fascinating consequence of supernova explosions is that while the outer layers of the star are expelled, the stellar core collapses, forming a neutron star or, in the case of the most massive exploding stars, a black hole. Research on these two types of objects, which lies outside the scope of this book, has fascinated both astronomers and the general public.

The material released in supernova explosions, added to the gas already between the stars, reproduces in a general way the chemical composition of the solar atmosphere, most stars, and the interstellar gas—the so-called cosmic abundance. There are a number of important discrepancies, however. In particular, the light nuclei of odd electric charge, such as nitrogen (see table 1.1), cannot be made from helium nuclei; hence such elements are not produced much in a primordial, or first-generation, star, which was initially composed of hydrogen and helium only.

To obtain good agreement with the observed cosmic composition, we must take into account later generations of stars formed from gas enriched with heavy elements created in earlier generations. When a massive second-generation star is born, it will have an appreciable abundance of carbon, produced by first-generation massive stars and ejected into interstellar space. These carbon nuclei will capture protons during the hydrogen-burning phase in the second-generation star, forming appreciable amounts of nitrogen, which accounts for the relative abundance of this element in table 1.1. Also, in certain phases of its evolution, a massive star, when its outer regions have swollen to gigantic dimensions (forming a so-called giant star), becomes subject to flashes, or thermal pulses, in the helium-burning shell at the base of the helium zone (see figure 1.4). These brief pulses of high temperature may each produce a burst of neutrons. In a second-generation star these neutrons can be absorbed by iron and heavier nuclei that were produced in first-generation stars. The gradual evolution of heavy elements by the capture of neutrons formed in some such way must be added to the previous, very rapid capture of neutrons during an earlier supernova explosion, if we wish to explain the cosmic composition. A few nuclei are apparently produced in second-generation (or possibly even third-generation) supernovae, whose chemical composition before explosion included very heavy elements formed in stars of earlier generations.

Precise computations of chemical abundances must take into account, of course, the existence of isotopes, which, for simplicity, have been mostly ignored in the preceding discussion. Different isotopes of an element have nuclei with the same nuclear charge but different mass. Hence for each element the different nuclear isotopes will contain the same number of protons and will be able to attract and hold the same number of orbital electrons but will contain different numbers of neutrons. Deuterium, which is formed in the Big Bang, as pointed out above, is an isotope of hydrogen; its nucleus (a deuteron) consists of a neutron and a proton stuck together. The observed relative abundances of the different isotopes for each chemical element are accounted for in most details by the processes described above, especially by the successive capture of neutrons, first rapidly in the explosion of first-generation massive stars, then slowly in the second-generation stars that are formed subsequently. This close agreement is clearly a major triumph of stellar nucleogenesis theory.

Evidently this cosmic cycle of star formation, element generation, expulsion of heavy atoms back into interstellar space, followed again by star formation, has been responsible for producing the stuff of which all of us are made. In view of the relatively low abundances of elements heavier than helium, (see table 1.1), the amount of material processed in supernovae need be only a small fraction of the interstellar gas. The relative scarcity on Earth of hydrogen and helium results from the fact that these elements are generally gaseous and did not condense on to the small solid particles from which our Earth was formed.

## FROM SUPERNOVA BACK TO STAR

In the last stages of the cosmic cycle, the material ejected from the supernova expands into interstellar space, becomes mixed with the gas there, and condenses to form new stars. This stage is more complex and less well understood than either the Big Bang or the formation of elements in stars. The theory of the Big Bang is much simplified by the assumed uniformity of the newly created Universe, with all physical quantities independent of location at any time. Such a theory is one-dimensional (time being the one dimension) and relatively simple. The theory of stellar evolution and element formation is somewhat more complicated, since conditions in a star depend on distance from the center as well as time. Such a theory is two-dimensional (one spatial dimension and time), but if the equations are known, a modern computer can handle them.

By contrast, studies of the motions in the interstellar gas, including the expansion of a supernova remnant, mixing of the ejected material with the existing gas, and formation of new stars, are dominated by irregularities. The interstellar gas is clumpy to begin with, and the expanding supernova material, shot out at enormous velocities, sweeps away the low-density gas and compresses the preexisting clouds to higher densities, accentuating the clumpiness. Star formation depends on the evolution and condensation of clumps or clouds. In such irregular situations all physical quantities depend in a complex way on three physical dimensions as well as on the time and cannot yet be followed with a computer. Hence the discussion of these processes must be somewhat approximate, based on idealized, simplifying assumptions.

We follow first the expansion of the gas ejected by a supernova. We make the simplifying assumption that the interstellar medium is uniform, with a density equal to its average value of about one hydrogen atom per cubic centimeter. Since this interstellar density is so low, the supernova gas first moves outward unhindered, as though it were expanding into a vacuum. In time, typically about a hundred years after the explosion, the expanding gas, which has shot outwards by a few light years, has fallen to about the same low density as the interstellar gas, and interactions between these two gases have become significant. Atoms in the supernova gas, enriched in heavy elements, collide with those in the interstellar gas at very high velocities—thousands of kilometers per second. These velocities, whose initial values correspond to thermal motions at temperatures of some $10^{8°}$ K or more, are randomized (both in direction and magnitude) by the collisions. Astronomers use the name supernova remnant for this hot expanding shell of gas, even though, after the first hundred years, the remnant contains more swept-up interstellar gas than material from the exploding star. As the remnant continues to move outward, it slows down, and the temperature decreases. Finally, after a million years or so, the remnant will slow down to a typical interstellar velocity of some 10 km sec$^{-1}$, and will decrease in temperature.

Because of the irregularities mentioned above, the actual development of a supernova remnant is more complicated. Figure 1.5 is a photograph of such a remnant, seen in the constellation Vela. The filaments are thought to be produced by outward-moving shells of

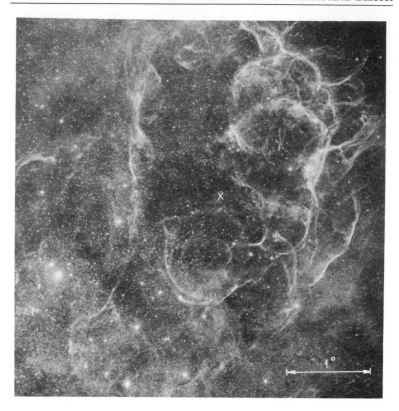

FIGURE 1.5 Supernova remnant in the constellation Vela. The x shows approximately where a star exploded some 10,000 years ago, forming a supernova. The gases, expanding at speeds of many thousands of kilometers per second, have formed a luminous remnant, whose whorls and loops are evident.

gas. Theoretical calculations show that the supernova producing this remnant exploded some 10,000 years ago. Later chapters discuss these remnants in more detail.

An important step in the cosmic cycle is the mixing of supernova material with the rest of the interstellar gas. If a supernova explosion were spherically symmetrical, with hot gas moving smoothly outward into a uniform iterstellar medium, no appreciable mixing would occur. Most of the interstellar gas would retain its primordial composition, remaing a mixture of hydrogen and helium only, while material shot out of supernovae would retain a very high enrichment of heavy elements. In fact, however, most newly formed stars have about the same composition as the Sun, indicating that the interstellar gas must have been mixed rather thoroughly. It seems that the irregularities that we find present in the interstellar gas are quite sufficient for substantial mixing.

As one might expect, this mixing was apparently less than perfect. Precise measurements of meteorites show small, subtle differences in their composition (especially in the relative abundances of different isotopes of various elements). These chunks of solid matter are bodies that have been travelling around the Sun for aeons and that finally collided with the Earth and were big enough to reach the ground without burning up. These differences in composition seem to be explicable only if the composition of the material that condensed to form the meteorites was different for different samples. Perhaps a number of different supernovae contributed to the gas in the solar system. In different regions small differences might be expected in the relative amounts of gas coming from these various sources of heavy elements.

The final step in the cosmic cycle is the formation of new stars, enriched in heavy elements produced by earlier stellar generations. One item of which we are sure in this connection is that stars are forming at the present epoch within our own Galaxy and in other spiral galaxies also. The evidence for this is the existence of some very luminous stars, with an intrinsic brightness exceeding that of the Sun by some $10^5$ to $10^6$. (The masses of these stars are at least twenty times that of the Sun.) There is no known source of energy that can maintain such a high energy output for as long as the Sun has been shining, which is a few billion years. At this enhanced rate of burning, the energy available from hydrogen fusion will last for some $10^6$ to $10^7$ years only. Evidently these very luminous stars must have started to shine only within the last few million years, and must have formed not much longer ago. By astronomical standards these stars are very young. As pointed out in the next chapter, such stars are generally located only in regions containing substantial amounts of interstellar gas, confirming that these very luminous, massive stars have formed recently from gas clouds.

Concerning the detailed process of star formation, we cannot be as definite as we would like. Gravitational instability and the process of fragmentation, discussed earlier in connection with galaxy formation, presumably play an important part. After our present knowledge of the interstellar medium has been summarized, we shall return in the final chapter to this fascinating, but complex, topic.

We may wonder as to the ultimate fate of this cosmic cycle. Someday this process must come to an end. Only a certain fraction of the gas condensing into new stars gets ejected back into interstellar space. Much of the gas forms stars that are considerably less massive than the Sun and that in time will die quietly, without expelling much matter (becoming at first white dwarfs, then cold, dark objects). As the gas in interstellar space gets used up in this way, it may be replenished by intergalactic matter, which can fall into galaxies, replacing gas that has become permanently locked up in low-mass stars. In time, however, even this source will become exhausted, and star formation will gradually draw to a close. By this time the Sun and other old stars will have cooled and faded, and except for very occasional, brief flashes of luminosity where stars have collided, as they surely must, the Universe will gradually become dark—a much less interesting place in which to live. However, this fate is perhaps $10^{11}$ years in the future, and the supplies of nuclear fuel (deuterium and uranium) in the planets themselves could maintain life for much of this period. So this prospect of ultimate darkness need not concern us immediately.

The Universe could end in a different way. If the average density of matter in the Universe is great enough (more than ten times higher than is now widely assumed), gravitational attraction will gradually halt the expansion, and contraction will start. After many billions of years, during which the cosmic temperature and density will steadily increase, the Universe will presumably contract again to an incredibly high density. After that, who knows? In any case, nothing material could survive the fiery holocaust of a Big Collapse.

As Robert Frost wrote:

Some say the world will end in fire
Some say in ice.
From what I've tasted of desire
I hold with those who favor fire.
. . . for destruction ice
Is also great
And would suffice.

# 2

# The Interstellar Medium as Viewed in 1970

A successful scientific endeavor is almost always an extension of previous results obtained by many other scientists. In this respect, progress in a field of science is like the construction of a highway into increasingly difficult terrain. A bridge built with great difficulty across a mountain chasm may be hailed as a great achievement, but it would not have been possible without the earlier stretches of highway, some of which required surmounting obstacles that were every bit as difficult in relation to the techniques available as those encountered later. Progress in science is a continuing group effort. Each advance relies heavily on what has gone before.

Thus, to understand the significance of results obtained in interstellar matter research during the decade 1970–80, we shall first examine the advances made prior to 1970. Since the very existence of a general interstellar medium was in doubt until about 1930, this survey will cover research only from 1930 to 1970. The principal results on interstellar matter obtained during this 40-year period were achieved first with visible light and then with radio waves at a wave length of 21 cm, which are emitted and absorbed by neutral hydrogen atoms.

Preceding the discussion of these results is a brief review of the way in which matter interacts with light waves, radio waves, and electromagnetic radiation in general. Astrophysics is mostly based on observation and interpretation of such radiation. To understand how this research can reveal the nature of the interstellar gas, we must know how atoms and electromagnetic waves interact with each other. Such knowledge is required to interpret the clues that Nature has provided in the radiation reaching the Earth. Readers who are already familiar with this material are advised to skip the following section.

## MATTER AND RADIATION

The interaction between matter and electromagnetic radiation is simplest for the hydrogen atom, with which we begin this discussion. This lightest atom consists of an electron moving in an orbit around a proton. We need not discuss here how the behavior of the electron is determined by its wavelike properties. The important result is that, because of these properties, the electron in the hydrogen atom can exist only in certain states.

These various states are characterized by different energies of the electron. The chief contribution to the electron energy, and the only one we shall consider in this introductory survey, is the electrical attraction of the proton for the electron. The possible states can be visualized as possible orbits for the electron as it moves around the proton. The orbit in which the electron has the smallest average distance from the proton is the orbit of lowest energy, which is the *ground state* of the hydrogen atom. If the atom is left quietly to itself for a few moments, it will inevitably emit some radiant energy spontaneously and end up in this ground state. Other possible states correspond to a variety of orbits, some circular, some elliptical, all characterized by greater average distances from the proton than that for the ground state. These more remote orbits are all said to correspond to *excited states*. The more excited the state, the greater the energy and the greater the average distance of the electron from the proton. An atom in the ground state is said to be *unexcited*. This distinction between ground states and excited states will subsequently be basic for us.

An electron will usually not remain in an excited state for more than a brief interval—typically $10^{-8}$ seconds, which, although it is a very short time, is enormously longer than the $10^{-15}$ seconds required for an electron in the first excited orbit to make one revolution around a proton. During this time interval of many orbits, an electron will generally move inward to an orbit closer to the proton with correspondingly lower energy. The electron may move to the ground state in one jump, or it may reach this state in several successive moves. Each such move, or *transition*, from an excited state to a less excited one is accompanied by the spontaneous emission of electromagnetic radiation. We have already noted in the discussion of the Big Bang that the emission of such radiation always occurs in a bundle or packet of waves, called a photon. In general each spontaneous transition of an atom from an excited state to a less excited state produces one photon which moves away at the speed of light $(3 \times 10^5$ km sec$^{-1}$).

The greater the energy, $E$, released by a transition between two states, the shorter the wavelength, $\lambda$, of the resulting photon. (The two are related by Planck's law, $E = hc/\lambda$, where $c$ is the speed of light, and $h$ is Planck's constant.) Thus transitions between states with little difference in energy produce photons of infrared or radio waves. Other transitions can release much larger energies, producing ultraviolet or X-ray photons (see figure 3.1).

The photons produced by a transition between two particular states will all have the same wavelength (as is required by energy conservation and Planck's law). Transitions between different pairs of states produce photons of different wavelengths, corresponding to different photon energies. Physicists have developed theories that predict very precisely the wavelengths of the radiation emitted by hydrogen atoms. The important point for astronomers is that atoms in each excited state emit photons of known wavelengths and only these particular photons.

Although this restriction of photon emission to particular wavelengths has been described here for hydrogen, it is in fact valid for other atoms also, and even for molecules (which are composed of several atoms bound together). In these more complicated systems, in which many electrons are moving around, the particle orbits and their energies are difficult to compute theoretically from basic physical laws. Hence the wavelengths of the photons emitted in each particular transition can usually not be calculated precisely from first principles. However, these wavelengths can be measured, and again it is found that an atom or molecule in a particular excited state can emit photons only of certain particular wavelengths, each such wavelength corresponding to one type of transition from an initial state to some less excited state of lower energy.

This discovery by spectroscopists many years ago has been a vital cornerstone of modern astrophysics. By measuring the wavelengths of photons emitted from excited atoms and molecules in distant regions of the Universe, astrophysicists can determine the chemical elements present, their states of excitation, and their velocities. The photons that have travelled for many years through nearly empty space are messengers that bring us information on the chemical composition and physical state of the gas that gave them birth.

Absorption of photons is about as important astronomically as emission. In the absorption process, a passing photon excites one of the atomic electrons, which moves to a more excited state—that is, a state of higher energy; the photon disappears and is said to have been absorbed. What has happened is that the energy of the photon has been transformed into the increased energy of the electron in the atom.

Since absorption of a photon is simply the process of emission run backward, the wavelengths of photons that can be emitted by atoms of a particular type are also the wavelengths of photons that can be absorbed. Emission requires that the atom be excited in some way, usually by thermal collisions with other atoms or free electrons; absorption requires that radiation from some source shine through the atoms, thereby providing photons that can be absorbed; a distant star can serve as such a light source.

Finally, let us consider how astronomers use telescopes to detect the emission and absorption of photons in gas at vast distances from the Earth. A spectrometer is an instrument designed to measure the amount of electromagnetic energy coming down the telescope tube at each of many wavelengths. Since the wavelength of a photon can never be measured with complete accuracy, we cannot measure the wave energy at exactly some wavelength. Instead we must measure the energy received within some narrow band of wavelengths; that is, in some narrow region of the spectrum, which we shall refer to as the "measurement band." If we make a graph of the radiant energy received—the *intensity*—for different values of λ, the wavelength at the center of the particular measurement band, we obtain results similar to those in figure 2.1. If such a plot extends over all measurable wavelengths, it is called the *spectrum* of the radiation received. Each of the plots in figure 2.1 shows only part of the spectrum. At this scale, the full spectrum would extend for a hundred meters or more.

In figure 2.1 diagram A shows an emission spectrum, such as might be obtained from an interstellar cloud of hot, excited gas. The narrow wavelength regions where strong emission is evidently present are called *emission features* of the spectrum. (For historical reasons, associated with the way a spectrum can be recorded photographically, scientists usually refer to emission features as *emission lines*.)

Diagram B shows the effects that absorbing atoms will produce when placed in the light path between an observer and a source of light with a *continuous spectrum*. In a source of this type (see p. 55), such as a very hot furnace or a dense star with a high surface temperature, the spectrum shows no emission or absorption features be-

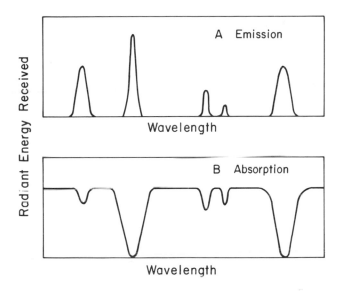

FIGURE 2.1 Emission and absorption spectra. The upper diagram, A, shows a narrow wavelength region of an emission spectrum produced by a hot gas. The lower diagram, B, shows the absorption spectrum formed in the same wavelength region when light from a source with a continuous spectrum passes through a cool gas containing the same atoms that produced the emic sion spectrum. The right-hand absorption feature shows shallow extensions, or wings, on each side.

fore the radiation passes through the intervening gas. Over the short wavelength range depicted in diagram B, a continuous spectrum is very nearly a straight horizontal line, indicating that the number of photons received per second is the same at all wavelengths within the range plotted. When light from such a source passes through an intervening gas, the wavelength regions where photons have been absorbed by atoms or molecules are called *absorption features* (or *absorption lines*). Note how the central wavelength of each absorption feature in diagram B is identical with that of the corresponding emission feature in A.

The widths of most astronomical emission and absorption features, such as those shown in figure 2.1, result usually from motions along the line of sight. If an atom is moving away from us (or toward us), the wavelength of the photon that it emits toward us appears shifted to longer (or shorter) wavelengths by the Doppler effect. The relative wavelength shift (defined as the increase in wavelength, $\Delta\lambda$, divided by the initial wavelength, $\lambda$) equals $v/c$, where $v$ is the velocity of recession, often called the *radial velocity*, and $c$ is the velocity of light (expressed in the same units as $v$). For motions within our Galaxy, $v$ is usually much much less than $c$, and the wavelength shift produced by the Doppler effect, which we call the *Doppler shift*, is small but measurable.

There are two important ways in which Doppler shifts can broaden an absorption or emission feature: by random atomic motions and by stellar rotation. Thermal velocities of atoms are random, with velocities of approach and recession equally likely. Hence an absorption or emission feature will be broadened by Doppler shifts due to thermal motion. If the gas as a whole is moving either toward or away from us, there is also a Doppler shift of the line center. In a rotating star, one edge will be approaching us, and in the spectrum received from this edge, any absorption features will be shifted to shorter wavelengths. The other edge will be receding from us, producing a Doppler shift to longer wavelengths. When the spectrum of the star as a whole is viewed, any absorption features will therefore be widened. Since the velocity of rotation near the equator of a star can be as great as several hundred kilometers per second—more than ten times greater than the random thermal velocities in most gas clouds between the stars—stellar absorption features can be much wider than most interstellar ones.

There is another effect besides the Doppler shift that sometimes produces rather broad absorption features. An atom is capable of weak absorption at wavelengths that differ from the central wavelength of the feature by substantially more than the usual Doppler shifts. As a result, if the absorption feature is extremely strong—that is, if there are unusually many absorbing atoms along the line of sight to the luminous source—the feature will show extended *wings*, as indicated in the right-hand feature of diagram B in figure 2.1.

Although analysis of emission and absorption spectra is the fundamental technique around which much of astrophysics has developed, this procedure has its limitations. One fundamental limitation is that an emission spectrum gives no direct information on the distance of the emitting atoms. Any distance may be assumed. With an absorption spectrum, there is some limited information on location, since the absorbing atoms must be somewhere between us and the source of the radiation that is being absorbed. For either emission or absorption, the strength of a particular feature depends only on the number of emitting or absorbing atoms that lie along the line of sight from the telescope through the gas involved. This number is independent of whether the atoms are close to us, far away, or distributed over a range of distances.

Uncertainty in the distance of atoms producing an absorption feature leads to the possibility of confusion between stellar and interstellar features. Very few stars have truly continuous spectra. The spectra of most stars used as light sources for measuring interstellar absorption features also show numerous absorption features produced by atoms in the cooler stellar atmospheres overlying the hotter radiating layers. Usually the interstellar features can be identified in one of two ways. Such features tend to be narrow, with widths of less than an Ångstrom (1 Å or Ångstrom unit = $10^{-8}$ cm). Stellar features are often much wider, with widths of several Ångstroms, as a result of Doppler shifts produced by stellar rotation. Also, some interstellar features are produced by atoms that are relatively very scarce in the atmospheres of the hot stars used as light sources; neutral atoms are a good example, since most atoms are ionized one or more times in a stellar atmosphere at a temperature of 20,000°K or more. With a careful choice of either absorbing atoms or source stars, features can be found that are certainly produced by atoms between the stars.

## RADIO EMISSION AND ABSORPTION BY HYDROGEN

Hydrogen has an important emission feature at radio wavelengths. This feature exists because of a very small contribution to the electron energy produced by the spins of the electron and the proton. As a result, when the electron in a hydrogen atom is in the orbit of lowest energy, it may be in either of two states. In one, the true ground state, the electron and proton are spinning in opposite directions. In the other, which is the first excited state, the spins are in the same direction, and the energy is very slightly greater, as a result of magnetic effects associated with these rotating charges; this excitation energy is enormously less that the energy associated with the first excited orbit.

A transition between these two states of opposite electron spin can occur spontaneously. The wavelength of the emitted photon is 21 cm, in the region of short-wavelength radio waves. This transition was predicted theoretically in 1945 by the Dutch astronomer H. C. van de Hulst, who pointed out the potential importance of this emission feature in interstellar matter research. Since then the hydrogen emission feature at 21 cm has been observed extensively by many astronomers.

The great advantage of the 21-cm feature is that it permits observations throughout the Galaxy of hydrogen, the dominant constituent of the interstellar gas. At these radio wavelengths the Galaxy is relatively transparent, and 21-cm photons emitted from the other side of our disc-shaped system, at a distance of some 50,000 light years, can readily be detected. By contrast, the small solid particles, or dust grains, that are also found between the stars, absorb visible light. As a result, photons emitted from the center of the Galaxy at visible wavelengths do not reach us at all.

A major discovery based on 21-cm emission measurements is that the average particle density of atomic hydrogen in the galactic plane at the Sun's distance from the galactic center is about 0.7 atoms per cubic centimeter. As we shall see in chapter 4, ultraviolet data yield a somewhat greater value for the hydrogen particle density in the galactic plane within 3,000 light years of the Sun.

Since this density determination is important in many discussions of what happens in interstellar space, we outline here the principal steps that are involved. The intensity of 21-cm photons received from a certain direction depends only on the particle *column density* of emitting hydrogen atoms, a quantity denoted by N(H). Quantitatively, N(H) is defined as the total number of hydrogen atoms in a long, thin cylinder with a cross-sectional area of 1 cm², extending indefinitely far along the line of sight. Hence N(H) is expressed in units of hydrogen atoms per square centimeter—that is, per unit area of the cylinder's cross-section. Since there is generally no confusion of particle column density with mass column density, we shall usually omit the word *particle* and refer to N(H) as the column density of neutral hydrogen atoms. From detailed measurements of the emission spectrum of 21 cm, a straightforward (but somewhat approximate) calculation gives N(H) for each direction in which the telescope is pointed.

In interpreting such data, one might worry that the observed 21-cm emission might come from hydrogen atoms outside our Galaxy, perhaps billions of light years away. Fortunately this possibility can be ruled out. Any stellar system outside our own will generally be moving away from us at a high velocity, typically much exceeding a thousand kilometers per second. Any 21-cm photons emitted by hydrogen atoms in such a system will be strongly shifted in wavelength due to the Doppler effect and will be well separated in wavelength from the 21-cm emission feature from our own Galaxy; the width of this feature corresponds to a velocity spread of at most a few hundred kilometers per second. Thus the column density obtained clearly includes only those hydrogen atoms within our Galaxy.

To compute an average particle density of hydrogen atoms, we must estimate the length, L, of the cylinder in which the emitting atoms are found. Then, dividing N(H), the number of hydrogen atoms in the cylinder, by the length, L (the volume equals L, since the cross-sectional area is 1 cm²) gives the average particle density. The values of N(H) range from about $10^{20}$ to $10^{23}$ cm$^{-2}$, the higher values being obtained in the direction of the galactic plane, the lower values in a nearly perpendicular direction. (By comparison, this range of column densities for oxygen and nitrogen molecules in the air around us is found for values of the path length, L, between 4 cm and 40 m.)

To determine the path length, L, through the emitting region of the galactic disc, we make use of the known dimensions of the disc—namely the diameter, which is about $10^5$ light years, and the thickness, which is some $10^3$ light years. For the different directions in which N(H) has been determined, L can be estimated from the geometry, and an average value of n(H), the hydrogen particle density, can be determined. In this way the value of 0.7 hydrogen atoms per cubic centimeter referred to above was obtained for gas at the Sun's distance—about 25,000 light years—from the galactic center. Obviously these emission measurements cannot tell us just where along the line of sight the emitting atoms are located. As a result the actual particle density at any location may differ greatly from the average value.

Another set of important results obtained by means of 21-cm studies concerns the velocities of atoms in the interstellar hydrogen gas. We have seen that the emission feature at 21 cm is broadened by the Doppler effect associated with different atomic velocities of approach or recession. The observed broadening of the emission feature may be used to determine the relative numbers of emitting atoms moving at different velocities.

To illustrate this effect, figure 2.2 shows a 21-cm emission feature observed in the galactic plane in the direction of the constellation Perseus (at a galactic longitude of 116°). As we saw earlier, the measured radiant energy within each measurement band, arriving from some area in the sky, is called the *intensity;* if the spectrum shows emission only, as in figure 2.2, the measurement gives the *emission intensity.* The 21-cm feature plotted in this figure shows two distinct

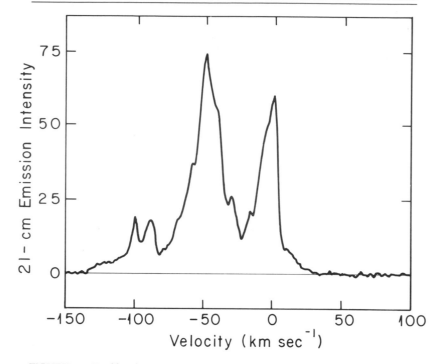

FIGURE 2.2 Profile of 21-cm emission from the galactic plane in Perseus. The intensity of 21-cm emission radiation is plotted against the radial velocity, $v$ (related to the observed wavelength by the Doppler effect). The radio telescope is pointed toward Perseus. The gas that emits at $v=0$ is in the local Orion arm surrounding the Sun; the gas emitting at $v = -50$ km sec$^{-1}$ is in the Perseus arm, at a distance of about 7,000 light years.

peaks, one centered at $v=0$, the other, at $v = -50$ km sec$^{-1}$, where $v$ is the velocity of the emitting atoms. (These radial velocities have been corrected both for the Earth's velocity of 30 km sec$^{-1}$ around the Sun and for the Sun's motion of 20 km sec$^{-1}$ through the neighboring stars. Thus the interstellar velocities given here and elsewhere in this book are relative to the center of gravity of the stars in the solar neighborhood.)

To interpret these results, we must, as often happens, introduce evidence obtained from two other areas of astronomy. First, observations of hot, young, massive stars in our Galaxy show that such stars are concentrated in vast elongated structures called *arms* by analogy with the spiral arms of other galaxies (see figure 1.3). The

Sun is located in one of these structures, called the Orion arm. Another, called the Perseus arm, is about 5,000 light years further from the galactic center. Second, measures of stellar radial velocities show that the disc of the Galaxy is rotating not as a solid body, but differentially, with a shorter rotation period at distances close to the galactic center. Partly because of this type of rotation, and partly because of other large-scale motions, different regions of the Galaxy have appreciably different radial velocities. The radial velocities of the stars in the Perseus arm have been measured from the Doppler effect of the absorption features produced in their atmospheres. The average velocity of these stars with respect to the Orion arm, measured in the same direction as figure 2.2, is about equal to the difference of 50 km sec⁻¹ shown there between the two peaks.

Thus we see that the interstellar hydrogen gas moves with the stars, suggesting that the gas is concentrated in the regions in which bright, young stars are found. The close association of young stars and gas in the spiral arms of other galaxies was pointed out in chapter 1. It is difficult to establish conclusively that such an association exists in our own Galaxy, just as it is difficult for a person in a forest to view the forest as a whole, because the trees on all sides get in the way. However, this evidence of the 21-cm emission from the Perseus arm provides important support for this association, tending to confirm that young stars in our Galaxy form from interstellar gas.

The density of gas in the region between the Orion and Perseus arms may be less than is implied by the rather modest dip in 21-cm radiation between the two peaks in figure 2.2. Atoms at radial velocities between the two peaks may actually be located in either of the two arms, since it is known that within each arm some clouds, or regions of gas, have large random velocities with respect to neighboring regions. The most detailed evidence for cloud velocities is obtained from visible absorption features, discussed below.

Measurements of 21-cm emission from the Perseus arm can also be used to determine the thickness of the hydrogen disc, with the use of simple trigonometry. Observations of the emitting region in the same general direction as figure 2.2 show an angular extent of about 4° on each side of the galactic plane. Since the tangent of 4° is 0.070, and the distance of the Perseus arm from the Sun (again measured in the same direction) is about 7,000 light years, it follows that the galactic hydrogen layer extends 490 light years on each side of the galactic plane, giving a total thickness of about 1,000 light years, comparable to the thickness of the stellar galactic disc.

The last 21-cm results to be discussed here concern the temperature of the hydrogen gas. These results are based on the physical principle that for these transitions involving such small changes in energy—much less than the mean thermal energy of the gas particles—the absorbing power of a hydrogen atom for 21-cm radiation varies inversely with the gas temperature, $T$. (With increasing temperature, the stimulated emission tends to cancel the absorption more completely.) Thus, when the fraction of radiation at 21 cm absorbed in a hydrogen cloud is small, as is usually the case, this fraction is proportional to $N(H)/T$, where $N(H)$ is again the column density as defined above (p. 32). Thus $T$ is proportional to $N(H)$ divided by the fraction of 21-cm radiation absorbed along the line of sight through the emitting atoms.

To make use of this relationship, and thus determine the gas temperature, two requirements must be met. In the first place $N(H)$ must be known; as we have already seen, this column density of hydrogen atoms may be calculated from the observed 21-cm emission. In the second place there must be a continuous source of radio waves present, more distant than the emitting atoms, so that radiation from the source can be absorbed by the intervening atoms, producing an absorption feature in which the fraction of radiation absorbed, or relative absorption, can be measured. Nature has kindly provided such sources in the form of certain extragalactic objects that radiate powerfully at radio wavelengths and have continuous spectra. Many of these radio stars are so-called quasi-stellar objects, or quasars, with red shifts so large that blue light is shifted all the way into the infrared. The understanding of these objects is in itself a fascinating problem in astronomy, but to us they are simply bright, pointlike sources of radio waves, whose 21-cm radiation is absorbed by hydrogen atoms in our Galaxy.

We consider now the detailed procedures involved in the determination first of $N(H)$, and then of the relative absorption. In principle, the column density can be determined from the 21-cm spectrum of the radiation emitted by the intervening clouds of hydrogen—that is, from the cloud emission spectrum. This spectrum cannot be measured directly in the line of sight to a bright source, however, because of interference by the source. Instead, the 21-cm emission is measured from several directions adjacent to the source, excluding the source itself. Normally the telescope is pointed in four directions slightly away from the source, first north, then east, then south, then west. The bright source does not affect the spectra measured in these directions, which show 21-cm emission from galactic gas clouds. If these emission spectra are in reasonable agreement, their average should be nearly equal to the spectrum of the radiation emitted by hydrogen atoms in the Galaxy along the line of sight to the source. The upper diagram in figure 2.3 was obtained in this way. The plot of 21-cm emission represents an average over directions adjacent to the radio source 3C237 (the designation for source no. 237 in the third Cambridge catalog of such sources). Since the emission at 21 cm depends only on the total number of emitting hydrogen atoms in the line of sight, and not on their temperature, such emission data give approximately the column density of hydrogen atoms in our Galaxy in the direction of the radio source. (Since this particular source is 47° above the galactic plane, the column density of hydrogen atoms in the line of sight and the resultant 21-cm emission intensity are substantially less than those shown in figure 2.2, from measurements in the plane of the galactic disc.)

The second step in the determination of the gas temperature from 21-cm data is the measurement of radiation from the source, and in particular, determination of the relative absorption in the 21-cm feature produced by intervening hydrogen atoms in our Galaxy. For this purpose the telescope is pointed right at the source, and the intensity is measured at different wavelengths. The radiation emitted by galactic hydrogen atoms in this direction will also be included, but this emission intensity has already been measured in adjacent directions, and the average value is subtracted to give $I$, the true intensity of radiation from the source. At wavelengths somewhat greater or smaller than the central wavelength for the 21-cm feature, $I$ has the constant value, $I_c$, as shown in the lower diagram of figure 2.3, since the source has a continuous spectrum. The ratio of $I$ to $I_c$, called the relative intensity and denoted by $r$, is plotted in this diagram. Within the absorption feature, $r$ falls below 1; $1 - r$ is the relative absorption, which is sometimes called the depth of the absorption feature. The measured value of $1 - r$ can be combined with N(H), obtained from the emission data, to give the temperature $T$. (Quantitatively $T = KN(H)/(1 - r)$, where $K$ is a known physical constant.

As usual, complications arise when the technique is applied to actual data. In practice, both the emission and absorption features, when plotted against wavelength (or atomic velocity, using the Doppler-effect formula), are not the simple symmetrical features shown in figure 2.1. This is very evident in figure 2.3, where the emission and absorption features not only have complex shapes but also have quite different profiles from each other. Evidently, two absorption components are present along the line of sight, with velocities of 0 and 3 km sec$^{-1}$. These components are also seen in the emis-

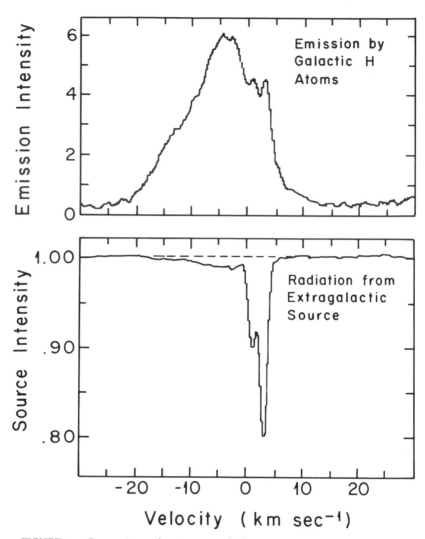

FIGURE 2.3 Comparison of emission and absorption spectra at 21 cm. The upper curve gives the average 21-cm emission spectrum from galactic hydrogen, averaged over directions adjacent to the radio source. The lower curve gives the spectrum of the extragalactic source, showing the absorption produced by galactic hydrogen atoms along the line of sight. To obtain the vertical scale for the extragalactic source, values of the intensity, $I$, have been divided by $I_c$, the intensity of the continuous radiation in the radio source spectrum, represented by the dashed line; this fraction is the relative intensity, r. The horizontal wavelength scale has been converted to the radial velocity of the hydrogen atoms by means of the Dopper-effect formula.

sion profile, but they are much weaker than the broad emission centered at about $-5$ km sec$^{-1}$; the corresponding absorption at this velocity is relatively weak. The physical explanation of this situation is that a variety of different clouds are drifting between the stars. Each cloud has a different velocity and a different gas temperature, as well as a different hydrogen column density along the line of sight through the cloud. Emission and absorption by all these clouds produce the complex profiles observed.

To analyze such situations, we split the data into velocity bands 1 km sec$^{-1}$ wide and analyze each band separately. Some thirty such bands are required to cover the full profiles in figure 2.3. The emission intensity gives N(H) for hydrogen atoms with velocities in each of these thirty bands, while the source intensity gives the relative absorption in each band. The ratio of these two determines the gas temperature for hydrogen atoms with velocities in each band.

(More quantitatively, we let $N(H, v_i)$ be the column density of hydrogen atoms whose radial velocity lies within $\pm 0.5$ km sec$^{-1}$ of the value $v_i$, the median velocity of the $i$th velocity band. If $I(v_i)$ is the measured source intensity at the Doppler-shifted wavelength corresponding to $v_i$, and $I_c$ is the source intensity at wavelengths outside the absorption feature, as before, then $I(v_i)/I_c$ is the relative intensity, $r(v_i)$, at each velocity $v_i$ and is reduced below 1 because of absorption by atoms within the velocity band centered at $v_i$. If $T_i$ is the temperature of these atoms, then $1 - r(v_i) = KN(H,v_i)/T_i$. The depth, or relative absorption, $1 - r(v_i)$, is here taken to be appreciably less than 1, which is usually the case.)

We now apply these concepts to the interpretation of the data in figure 2.3, obtaining information on the temperature of the hydrogen atoms whose velocities lie within each band. It will be seen that the emission intensity at velocities between $-9$ and $-10$ km sec$^{-1}$ is about as strong as between 0 and 1 km sec$^{-1}$ indicating that there are about the same number of emitting hydrogen atoms in these two ranges. However, the absorption in the former velocity band is about one-tenth of its value in the latter, indicating a tenfold difference in gas temperature between these two velocities; the gas with the weaker absorption is hotter. More detailed computations for this particular line of sight show that the gas with a radial velocity between $-9$ and $-10$ km sec$^{-1}$ (that is, with a velocity of approach between 9 and 10 km sec$^{-1}$) has an average temperature of about 500° K, while the gas receding from us with a velocity between 0 and 1 km sec$^{-1}$ has an average temperature of only about 50° K. The presence of strong emission in the upper diagram (at $v = -10$ km sec$^{-1}$) and relatively little absorption ($r \approx 1$) at the same velocity in the lower diagram is a striking feature of figure 2.3 and a strong indication that warm hydrogen gas is present.

The temperatures obtained from extensive analyses of such data show a wide range of variation. The clouds that absorb relatively strongly at 21 cm are relatively cool, with temperatures between 50 and 100° K. The less absorbing clouds are usually much hotter, with temperatures often greater than 1,000° K; such high temperatures are not well determined, because the absorption becomes very small and is difficult to measure precisely. The relatively high values for the temperatures were somewhat controversial when first obtained; however, both the low and the high values have now been fully confirmed by ultraviolet measurements, discussed in chapters 5 and 6. The temperatures of the interstellar gas have the same significance as the temperature of the air around us; they describe the energy of random motion of the atoms (and molecules) in the gas.

A fringe benefit of these extensive 21-cm absorption measures is that they provide an estimate of the amount of neutral hydrogen along a line of sight through a single cloud. The average value of the column density, $N(H)$, found in this way is $3 \times 10^{20}$ cm$^{-2}$. A cloud of about this column density is often called a *diffuse cloud*. Such clouds are also seen in 21-cm emission, though smaller clouds with substantially less gas ("cloudlets") and much more extended emitting regions are also seen.

## ABSORPTION OF VISIBLE LIGHT BY HEAVY ELEMENTS

There are two ways in which elements heavier than helium can interfere with starlight and thus reveal to us their presence in interstellar space. Condensed into small solid particles, they can intercept photons of any wavelength. In gaseous form, as free atoms, they can absorb photons of particular wavelengths, in the manner discussed above. By 1970, research on these two interstellar effects, using visible light, had given appreciable information, which we shall now survey.

Solid particles, or dust grains, can impede a passing photon, either absorbing it entirely or deflecting it somewhat in its flight; this second process is called *scattering*. In either case a beam of photons from a distant star will be weakened. Clouds of dust in the planes of distant spiral galaxies produce the dark bands evident in figure 1.3. Within our Galaxy the absorption and scattering produced by dust clouds produces the dark patches evident in figure 2.4. Even as late

FIGURE 2.4 Dust lanes and globules. The luminous gases in the Rosette nebula are heated and excited by radiation from hot, bright stars nearby. In some regions intervening dark clouds containing tiny dust particles as well as cold gas absorb the light. Photograph obtained with the 48-inch Schmidt telescope.

as 1900, some astronomers believed that such patches might be actual holes in the distribution of stars.

Evidence that these apparent holes are in fact produced by dust is obtained from the spectra of stars within or behind the clouds. The absorption and scattering of light by solid particles does not show the narrow absorption features characteristic of free atoms and molecules. However, the effectiveness of a grain in weakening or extinguishing light does vary smoothly with the wavelength of the light. This effectiveness is systematically less for wavelengths that are longer than the particle diameters than it is for shorter wavelengths. It so happens that the interstellar grains, which are very tiny, have diameters roughly equal to the average wavelength of visible light. As a result, obscuration of starlight by grains is greatest in the blue and ultraviolet regions of the spectrum, where the wavelength is less than the size of the grain; the obscuration is substantially less in the red and approaches zero in the infrared, where the wavelength becomes much greater than the grain dimensions. Thus a star whose light has been weakened by grains will also be reddened; that is, the ratio of the numbers of stellar photons observed at red and blue wavelengths will exceed its value for unobscured stars. Similarly the Sun appears reddened when it shines through a cloud of smoke particles. Astronomers have devised techniques for measuring such reddening precisely. The amount of reddening depends on the column density of the obscuring solid matter between us and the star being measured, as well as on the optical properties of a typical solid grain.

These measurements may be used to determine some of the physical properties of the interstellar dust. The average density of this material is of particular interest. While the observed obscuration of starlight is very patchy, an average over the plane of the Galaxy within a distance of 3,000 light years gives a smoothed density for dust of about $10^{-26}$ gm cm$^{-3}$. This is the density that would result if all the atoms in each grain were distributed uniformly over distances of a hundred or so light years. The smoothed density for dust grains is computed for a specific composition of the grains (carbon compounds and silicates), but about the same result is obtained for other theoretically plausible chemical compositions. Hydrogen (and helium also) is not likely to condense as solid particles in interstellar space; thus the grains must be composed predominantly of heavy elements (including those from carbon to iron—see chapter 1).

To explain this average density of dust, we must assume that an appreciable fraction of all heavy atoms between the stars have condensed from the gas onto these solid particles. According to the composition determined for the solar system (see table 1.1), and believed to be typical of our Galaxy generally, one hydrogen atom per cubic centimeter corresponds to a mass density of about $3 \times 10^{-26}$ gm cm$^{-3}$ of heavy elements, three times the observed mass density in grains. Since the data from the Copernicus satellite also show that the mean density of interstellar hydrogen is about one hydrogen atom per cubic centimeter (see chapter 4) we conclude that about one atom in every three heavier than helium has condensed into solid particles. As we shall see in chapter 6, almost all atoms of some chemical elements have apparently condensed onto dust grains.

A basic result obtained from these reddening studies is that the dust is not uniformly distributed but is very clumpy. If the column density of grains along the line of sight to a star is divided by the distance from the Earth to the star, L, one obtains the average density of dust grains along this line of sight. (In this computation L is found from a comparison of the measured star brightness with the total luminosity, or candlepower, which can be estimated from the relative strengths of certain absorption features produced in the stellar atmosphere.) If the density of dust were uniform, measures for different stars, with different lines of sight, should all give the same average density. In fact, quite the contrary is observed. Some distant stars in the galactic plane that are several thousand light years away are almost entirely unreddened. Other stars, in directions only a few degrees away from these distant unreddened objects and within a few hundred light years of the Sun, are highly reddened. Some thirty years ago analysis of these nonuniformities in more than a thousand stars showed that the dust tends to be concentrated in separate clouds, with each line of sight in the galactic plane intersecting an average of two or three such clouds per 1,000 light years. A random distribution then gives no clouds at all in 1,000 light years along some lines of sight and more than the average along others. This cloudy structure is fundamental to our understanding of the interstellar gas. The amount of material in one of these dust clouds is discussed in chapter 4.

Next we consider the absorption of visible light by heavy interstellar atoms in the gaseous state. As we shall see in the next chapter, most atoms between the stars cannot absorb visible light at all. The few atoms which do absorb such radiation are mostly so scarce or are such weak absorbers that the absorption features which they produce are very weak and can be measured only with difficulty. There are only two atoms that produce sufficiently strong absorption in the visible region of the spectrum to permit intensive study by astronomers.

One is neutral sodium. (The chemical symbol, Na, is taken from the Latin name, *natrium*, for this element.) The other is singly ionized calcium (Ca$^+$), a calcium atom from which one electron has been removed. These atoms produce strong interstellar absorption features in the spectra of hot stars. Since sodium and calcium are highly ionized in stars of high surface temperature, there is little, if any, absorption by Na or Ca$^+$ there. The intrinsic stellar spectrum at these wavelengths is very nearly continuous, and any observed absorption features are therefore almost entirely interstellar.

Each of these two types of atoms produces a pair of absorption features. The Na atom absorbs yellow light at wavelengths of 5,890 and 5,896 Å. The Ca$^+$ pair of absorption features is in the violet, at roughly 3,950 Å. Figure 2.5 shows a plot of the 5,896-Å region in the spectrum of Epsilon Orionis (a conspicuous second-magnitude star in the constellation Orion—the middle of the three stars in Orion's belt). This plot of the Na absorption feature was obtained in 1969 by L. M. Hobbs, using instrumentation built specially to provide an extremely narrow measurement band (with a width of 0.01 Å). As in the lower diagram of figure 2.3, the intensities in the spectrum have

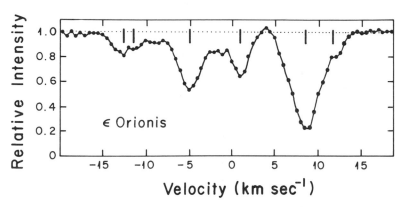

Velocity (km sec$^{-1}$)

FIGURE 2.5 Interstellar sodium absorption in Epsilon Orionis. The plotted points show the observed relative intensities in each 0.01-Å measurement band in the region of the neutral sodium absorption feature at about 5,896 Å. The horizontal wavelength scale has been converted to radial velocity by means of the Doppler-effect formula. The vertical lines above the spectrum indicate the six different components of the absorption feature; each component is the result of absorption by a group of atoms moving at the indicated velocity.

been divided by $I_c$, the intensity outside the absorption features, to give the relative intensity. The horizontal scale has been converted from Ångstroms to velocities in kilometers per second, using the normal Doppler-effect relation: $\Delta\lambda/\lambda = v/c$ (see p. 30). According to this relation, 0.5 km sec$^{-1}$ in the diagram corresponds to 0.01 Å.

Figure 2.5 shows separate absorption features at velocities of $-13$, $-12$, $-5$, $+1$, $+8$, and $+12$ km sec$^{-1}$ (again expressed with respect to the stars in the solar neighborhood). As in the discussion of the 21-cm absorption feature shown in figure 2.3, the Na absorption is said to possess separate components. It is customary to assume that each component, with its characteristic velocity, is produced by an interstellar cloud with that particular radial velocity, and that each different cloud is a physically distinct, separate entity. Indeed this is the simplest explanation, and the resultant picture of many separate clouds moving through interstellar space at random speeds, averaging some 10 km sec$^{-1}$, has dominated our thinking about the interstellar gas since 1949, when W. S. Adams published an extensive compilation of similar, though less precise results on components of interstellar Ca$^+$ in 300 stars. Adams obtained much of his observational material during World War II, when many astronomers were otherwise engaged and requests for observing time on the Mt. Wilson 100-inch telescope (then the world's largest) were relatively few!

From the observed absorption in these visual interstellar features, it is possible to determine the column densities of the absorbing atoms along the line of sight to each hot star whose spectrum shows these features. Unfortunately this information is not very helpful. Only a small, and uncertain, fraction of the interstellar sodium and calcium atoms are in the states that we can observe. These atoms are readily ionized by general starlight (for Na the energy required is 5.1 eV); when an ultraviolet photon is absorbed, the electron may acquire so much energy that it cannot be held by the atom in an excited state but goes off at a high velocity and moves freely through the gas. Most sodium interstellar atoms have lost one electron, becoming Na$^+$; most calcium atoms have lost two electrons, becoming Ca$^{++}$. Attempts have been made to compute from the column densities N(Na) and N(Ca$^+$) the overall densities of sodium and calcium atoms, including all stages of ionization, but the results have been somewhat uncertain, partly because the intensity of the radiation that ionizes these atoms is unknown. Hence visual absorption line studies give no really definitive information on the chemical composition of the interstellar gas. It seems plausible that the absorbing clouds of Na and Ca$^+$ are identical with those of hydrogen and dust discussed earlier. However, it was only with the *Copernicus* data (discussed in chapter 4) that this conclusion became firmly established.

## EMISSION FROM IONIZED REGIONS

While most interstellar hydrogen and helium gas in the Galaxy is in the form of neutral atoms, a small fraction—perhaps about ten percent—is in regions where most of these atoms have lost an electron, becoming ionized. In general an electron can be knocked off an atom either by absorption of a photon in the extreme ultraviolet (to ionize hydrogen requires 13.6 eV) or by collision with an energetic particle, especially a free electron with a velocity exceeding one percent of the speed of light. In some regions of the Galaxy, where particularly hot stars radiate strongly in the extreme ultraviolet, ionization of hydrogen and helium atoms is produced by the first of these two mechanisms; in other regions, surrounding exploding supernovae, by the second.

Near stars with high surface temperatures (30,000 to 50,000° K), the ultraviolet radiation is so intense that most atoms will be ionized. The atoms of hydrogen, and often of helium also, will tend to be completely stripped of their electrons, leaving bare nuclei, whereas heavy atoms will usually have lost from one to three electrons. A proton or heavy atomic ion will typically capture a free electron every thousand years or so but will normally lose it by photon absorption in roughly a year. The gas tends to be hot, and the heavy ionized atoms are excited by passing electrons once every few months. Since the excited electrons in an atom move down to the ground state in time intervals which are relatively short, the excitation does not last long, and at any one time almost all atoms are in the ground state.

As a result of emission by those few atoms that are excited, the hot stars, which as we have already seen are bright, massive, and relatively young, are surrounded by glowing envelopes of emitting gas. Downward transitions from one excited state to another produce photons of visible light, and these glowing, ionized regions can be seen by the eye through a telescope. Their visual spectra contain many emission features. One of the most conspicuous glowing regions of ionized gas is the Orion nebula (at the center of Orion's sword, due south of his belt). This nebula, which can be seen clearly with binoculars, surrounds the Trapezium, a group of four hot, young stars. Ultraviolet light from these stars ionizes and heats the gas in the nebula.

In addition, the gas in these regions emits radio waves, which can be detected on the Earth. Some atomic emission features at radio wavelengths are produced by electron transitions between highly excited states whose energies differ only slightly. Furthermore, free electrons colliding with ions emit continuous radiation, extending over the entire radio spectrum, a process discussed in the next chapter. These radio waves are not much affected by the solid particles, or dust grains, that produce such conspicuous absorption of visible light. Hence these ionized regions around hot stars can be detected by their radio emission (most conveniently at wavelengths between 10 and 50 cm), even when the visible and ultraviolet radiation from the stars themselves is completely obscured by dark intervening clouds.

These ionized regions around hot stars are probably better understood than any other component of the interstellar medium. The gas temperatures can be determined accurately from the relative intensities of various emission features and turn out to be about 8,000° K, in gratifyingly close agreement with what theorists predict. The proton particle density is found to have values ranging from 10 up to $10^3$ cm$^{-3}$, with even higher values in very small, compact regions. These ionized regions are generally at higher pressures than the gas that surrounds them and are typically expanding outward at speeds of 10 to 20 km sec$^{-1}$. This difference in pressure may compress any cold clouds engulfed in the exploding ionized gas. In any case, these ionized regions around hot, young stars provide important indicators of where such stars have formed recently. Like the hydrogen clouds that emit 21-cm radiation, these regions are generally found only in spiral arms of galaxies, providing additional confirmation that young stars form from the gas that is concentrated in these regions.

Now we turn away from the ionized gas surrounding bright, young stars to consider the hot gas ejected during supernovae explosions. Atoms in this gas become ionized by collisions with electrons, the second of the two ionizing processes mentioned above. We have already seen that the hot gases expelled from supernovae at speeds of thousands of kilometers per second become heated to enormous temperatures by mutual impact between the ejected gas and the surrounding interstellar medium. The outward-moving supernova remnant gradually cools and slows down as it sweeps up more and more of the surrounding interstellar gas. Since these hot remnants play an important part in the cosmic cycle (see chapter 1), some of their properties are summarized here.

From the very hot, rarefied gas in such remnants, no strong visible emission would be expected, nor is much observed. At temperatures exceeding $10^{6°}$ K, most oxygen atoms are stripped to bare nuclei. Recombination of electrons with such nuclei, or ions, produces some atoms in very highly excited states, which emit some visible photons in transitions to slightly less excited states. However, such recombination radiation is usually much too weak to detect. In a few remnants, weak emission features are seen, apparently produced by $Fe^{+13}$ ions—iron atoms from which 13 electrons have been stripped by collisions. Such stripping requires temperatures of several million degrees, in agreement with the temperatures expected theoretically in these remnants.

Most visible photons from supernova remnants are produced in dense, relatively cool clouds surrounded by hot gas, rather than in the hot gas itself. Some of these clouds have high velocities, either because the material was ejected in the supernova explosion or because it was accelerated by the hot gas rushing by. The most interesting clouds are those in the conspicuous supernova remnant in the constellation Cassiopeia. This supernova must have exploded between two and three hundred years ago but passed unnoticed at the time because of heavy obscuration by intervening dust clouds. The clouds within this remnant are of two types, intermediate-velocity and high-velocity. The intermediate-velocity clouds, moving at speeds of about 100 km sec$^{-1}$ (which is high compared with typical interstellar clouds), have normal emission spectra, with lines of hydrogen, nitrogen, and oxygen. Presumably these clouds were present before the supernova went off and had time to be accelerated only up to their modest, presently observed velocities.

The high-velocity clouds, moving with speeds between 4,000 and 8,000 km sec$^{-1}$, are of particular interest because of their unusual composition. Their spectra show no hydrogen, carbon, or nitrogen, but strong emission by oxygen and heavier atoms. This material was presumably shot out directly from the supernova, and, because of some irregularity in the explosion, formed separate, dense, and only moderately hot (about 30,000° K) clouds, rather than expanding in all directions. The ratios of hydrogen, carbon, and nitrogen in these clouds relative to oxygen are at most about one percent or less of their cosmic values (given in table 1.1). This composition is just what one would expect in those regions of massive stars where the hydrogen, helium, and carbon have all burned up. Thus these clouds provide direct confirmation that heavy elements are injected into the interstellar gas by stellar explosions.

X-rays should be the most prominent form of electromagnetic radiation produced by a very hot gas. As shown in table 3.1, X-ray photons are known to originate when a beam of electrons, accelerated across an electric potential of 10,000 Volts, for example, collide with stationary matter. Their wavelength is typically one ten-thousandth that of visible light (see figure 3.1). With "sounding rockets" shot above the atmosphere for a few minutes, X-rays have in fact been detected from a variety of supernova remnants; the photon energies observed correspond to electrons accelerated across potentials between 1,000 and 10,000 Volts. In the 1970s these measurements were made more precise by observations with increasingly powerful equipment placed on satellites.

Detailed theories of how these photons are produced indicate that the gas temperature in the older remnants ranges from roughly $3 \times 10^6$ to $7 \times 10^{6°}$ K. In remnants as young as the one in Cassiopeia, even higher temperatures are thought to be present in the low-density gas between the moving clouds. Since the effect of clouds and other nonuniformities was not systematically included in these early theories, some of the temperatures may be subject to revision. In any case, the X-ray observations show clearly that much of the outward-rushing gas in every supernova remnant must be extremely hot.

In addition to the X-rays observed from supernova remnants, a background of less energetic X-rays was observed, with photon wavelengths of about 50 Å. Such photons, which can be absorbed by interstellar hydrogen atoms, correspond to electrons accelerated across only 250 Volts. This radiation tends to be relatively weaker in directions near the galactic plane and somewhat stronger away from the plane, suggesting that it is produced by sources outside the galactic disc of absorbing hydrogen. In 1970 it was not clear whether such emission might be caused by an extended hot gas at a temperature of about $10^{6°}$ K or by a superposition of many faint point sources, each of which might resemble somewhat the known stellar sources of more energetic X-rays.

## SUMMARY

The 21-cm emission from neutral hydrogen atoms shows that the interstellar gas in the Galaxy is concentrated in a rotating disc some 1,000 light years thick. The total mass of the gas (mostly hydrogen and helium) in the galactic disc is comparable with the mass of the stars. A concentration of gas, dust and young, hot stars in the spiral arms of other galaxies is well established. Within the disc of our own Galaxy also, the hydrogen gas appears to be concentrated in regions where young stars have recently formed; these regions may be spiral arms in our system.

The observed absorption of starlight by hydrogen, calcium, and sodium atoms, as well as by dust grains, shows that these absorbing particles are concentrated in large numbers of separate clouds. The atomic clouds are moving through space with random speeds of some 10 km sec⁻¹.

The hydrogen 21-cm data indicate a wide range of gas temperatures. The absorbing clouds are at about 50 to 100° K; for hydrogen atoms seen mainly in emission the temperature is some ten to a hundred times higher. The sizes and compositions of different clouds, the fraction of the volume within the galactic disc that they occupy, and the nature of the material between them were not determined by studies before 1970.

In regions surrounding bright, young, hot stars, the hydrogen is ionized by ultraviolet stellar photons, which heat the gas to 8,000° K. Because of its high pressure the heated gas expands rapidly, with outward speeds of some 15 km sec⁻¹.

Around exploding stars, or supernovae, gas enriched in heavy elements is shot out at enormous speeds of thousands of kilometers per second. This exploding material sweeps up the surrounding interstellar gas, heating it to temperatures exceeding 10⁶° K, as indicated by the emitted X-rays.

# 3

# New Windows on the Universe

During the decade 1970–80 a number of fundamentally new observational tools became available for interstellar studies, thanks to the onward march of technology in general and the active U.S. space research program in particular. With these new techniques, observations were made in regions of the electromagnetic spectrum that had not been explored previously. In the present chapter, we will look at three of these new instruments and at the types of measurements that can be made with them. In later chapters, we will discuss some of the results that relate to the interstellar medium.

The first of these three instruments was the *Copernicus* satellite, which included a telescope-spectrometer specifically designed for observations of interstellar absorption features at ultraviolet wavelengths. The sweeping advances in our knowledge of the interstellar gas made possible by the *Copernicus* observations form a central focus of this book. The second important new advance in astronomical instrumentation was the development of detectors for radio waves of very short wavelength, between 0.1 and 1 cm. Observations in this *microwave* region of the spectrum have already provided significant new data on interstellar clouds and promise to be of increasing importance in the future. The third basically new observational development was the launching of several earth-circling satellites equipped with X-ray instruments. One experiment of particular importance for interstellar research is discussed in this chapter.

Before these developments in instrumentation are described, we shall review the different wavelength regions in the electromagnetic spectrum, pointing out how waves of each type are produced. This discussion sets in perspective the new windows that have been opened by the three instruments described in the later sections. Readers already familiar with this field of basic physics may wish to skip the following section.

## THE ELECTROMAGNETIC SPECTRUM

Electromagnetic radiation of any wavelength can exist. Such electromagnetic waves travel through a vacuum, always with the same speed, $c$, of $3 \times 10^5$ km sec$^{-1}$. A listing of the principal types of electromagnetic radiation, which together make up the electromagnetic spectrum, is given in figure 3.1.

Discussions of radio waves generally refer to the frequency, $\nu$, rather than the wavelength, $\lambda$, since in generating or receiving these waves it is the frequency of the tuned circuits that is controlled. Hence, for wavelengths longer than 0.1 cm, values of the frequency (given by $\nu = c/\lambda$) are listed in the third column of the figure. The basic frequency unit of one oscillation per second is called a Hertz (Hz).

For the shorter wavelengths, it is customary to specify photon energies rather than wavelengths. Hence in the lower part of the figure photon energies are listed in the third column. The unit of energy used is the *electron Volt* (eV), which is the energy gained by an electron when it is accelerated across an electric potential difference of 1 Volt. (For $E$ in eV and $\lambda$ in Å, Planck's law gives $E = 12,400/\lambda$.)

The wavelengths separating the different types of radiation are all arbitrary, excepting, of course, the range shown for visible light. Even here, the boundaries are somewhat different for different individuals, and many insects can see ultraviolet light. The other boundaries are mostly determined by differences in the methods of production or detection. For example, the distinction between infrared and microwaves is based on the method of detection; special amplifiers, tuned detectors, and associated hardware are used for most microwave frequencies, while infrared detectors normally measure directly the energy released in some solid material (which is usually cooled to a very low temperature to increase its sensitivity to small energy input). Between the extreme ultraviolet and longer ultraviolet waves, a major difference is that mirrors reflect very few photons of the shorter wavelengths except at grazing incidence. Thus, as instrumentation technology changes, some of the dividing lines between different types of radiation are altered.

The solid line to the right of the frequency and photon energy scale in figure 3.1 indicates roughly which electromagnetic waves do not reach the Earth's surface. Radiation from space with a wavelength exceeding 100 m is usually reflected back into space by the Earth's ionosphere. (Similar radio waves generated on the Earth are reflected back toward the Earth, improving reception in the broadcast

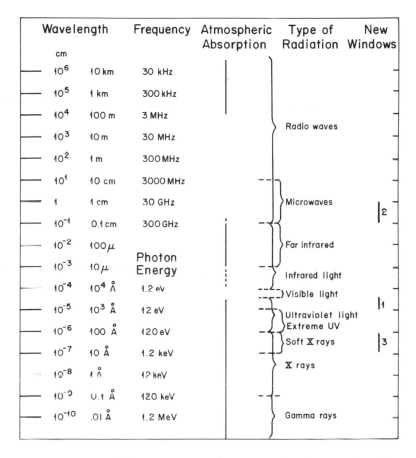

FIGURE 3.1 Types of electromagnetic radiation. Wavelengths are indicated on the left, in both centimeters (cm) and the units appropriate for each range of the spectrum—kilometers (km), meters (m), micrometers or microns (μ), and Angstroms (Å). Frequencies are shown for the longer wavelengths in units kilo-Hertz (kHz), mega-Hertz (MHz), and giga-Hertz (GHz), equal to $10^3$, $10^6$, and $10^9$ Hz, respectively. Similarly, photon energies, shown for the shorter wavelengths, are in electron-Volts (eV), kiloelectron-Volts (keV), and megaelectron-Volts (MeV). The solid line represents roughly those wavelengths where the atmosphere is strongly absorbing. The heavy lines at the far right show the wavelengths of the "new windows" that opened up during 1970–80.

band.) Radiation with a wavelength shorter than 0.1 cm is absorbed by atoms and molecules in the Earth's atmosphere, except for most of the band between 3,000 and 10,000 Å and a few narrow windows of transparency in the near infrared. (These windows, which are shown schematically in the figure, have been of vital importance for infrared research from telescopes on the ground.)

The space program has given astronomers the opportunity to make observations from above the atmosphere and thus to observe the entire electromagnetic spectrum, an enormous benefit for science. The early sounding rockets, which as we have already noted, spent only a few minutes above 100 km, have been followed by powerful scientific spacecraft in orbit around the Earth, detecting photons at a variety of wavelengths for periods ranging up to several years.

Table 3.1 indicates various physical processes that produce electromagnetic waves of different wavelengths. As in the case of the examples discussed here, these processes are the ones of particular importance for interstellar studies. In most wavelength regions, radiation can be produced by transitions between different states of atoms and

TABLE 3.1. Production of Electromagnetic Waves

| Type of Radiation | Source |
|---|---|
| Radio waves | Oscillating electrical circuits |
| | Hot ionized gas |
| | Energetic electrons in a magnetic field |
| Microwaves | Oscillations of electrons in vacuum tubes and various |
| (radio waves of | solid-state devices |
| short wavelength) | Transitions of atoms and molecules between states of |
| | almost identical energy |
| Infrared | Warm opaque material |
| | 1,000° K for 3 μ wavelength |
| | 300° K (27°C) for 10 μ wavelength |
| | 100° K for 30 μ wavelength |
| | Transitions of atoms and molecules between states of |
| | slightly different energy |
| Visible light | Hot opaque material |
| | 6,000° K for 5,000 Å wavelength |
| | Transitions of atoms and molecules between different |
| | excited states |
| Ultraviolet light | Hot opaque material |
| | 30,000° K for 1,000 Å wavelength |
| | Transitions between excited and ground states of |
| | atoms and molecules |
| X-rays | Target bombarded with energetic electrons |
| | Transitions between states of highly ionized atoms |
| | Hot ionized gas |
| Gamma rays | Transitions between states of an atomic nucleus |

molecules. As we have seen, the shortest wavelengths correspond to the largest energy differences, as for example, between the states of an atomic nucleus, whose excitation energies are measured in millions of electron Volts, while the longest ones correspond to very minute energy differences, such as $6 \times 10^{-6}$ eV for the excitation energy of the first excited state of hydrogen, which is responsible for emission and absorption by interstellar clouds at 21 cm. The photons produced or absorbed by these various transitions convey important astronomical information. It is only at the longer radio wavelengths that such transitions are relatively unimportant in astronomy, since the rates of emission and absorption rapidly decrease (as $1/\lambda^3$) with increasing wavelength, $\lambda$, and for $\lambda > 1$ m the number of photons absorbed or emitted is usually too small to observe.

As noted in the table, transitions to and from an atomic ground state usually involve absorption or emission of ultraviolet photons. This follows from a general property of excited states—namely, that the number of such states increases dramatically as the excitation energy becomes higher and higher. There are relatively few states of very low energy, and they tend to be widely spaced in energy. More highly excited states, with greater energy, are vastly more numerous and are much more closely spaced. Transitions between these highly excited states have low energy differences and emit (or absorb) visible or infrared photons. By contrast, in most atoms and also in hydrogen molecules, the excited states that can be reached by photon absorption from the ground state all have excitation energies of some 6 eV or more, corresponding to wavelengths less than 2,000 Å, well in the ultraviolet range. (The few exceptions to this rule among abundant atoms will be discussed in the next chapter.)

Another important process that produces electromagnetic waves is emission from opaque material, such as a solid body, at a uniform temperature. Radiation produced in this way is continuous—that is, the spectrum shows neither absorption nor emission features. As shown in table 3.1, at temperatures between 100 and 30,000° K, such emission is most intense at wavelengths between the far infrared and the ultraviolet. This process is astrophysically important, because the radiation from a star is roughly similar to that from an opaque body if the body has the same temperature as the visible layers of the star's surface. Thus the radiation from the Sun, with a surface temperature of about 6,000° K, is most intense, or peaks, at roughly 5,000 Å. Hotter stars, at a temperature of some 30,000°K, produce strong ultraviolet radiation, which provides the light source partially absorbed by interstellar atoms and observed from the Copernicus satellite.

Continuous radiation is also produced in a hot ionized gas (which produces emission features also, of course, if not all of the atoms are completely ionized). When there are few, if any, bound electrons revolving about positive nuclei, the continuous emission is produced by free electrons, which lose energy in random collisions with protons or other positive ions and radiate photons. This source of emission is not a very strong one, and in the microwave, infrared, and visible portions of the spectrum is usually masked by emission from other sources. However, in the radio emission from an ionized gas at about $10^{4°}$ K or in the X-ray emission from an ionized gas at about $10^{7°}$ K (both discussed in the previous chapter), this source can be the dominant one.

Another method listed for producing radio waves, the motion of a high-speed electron across a magnetic field, is important for explaining a number of astrophysical phenomena. A magnetic force acts on a moving electron, causing its path to deviate from a straight line and forcing it to move in a circular path. As viewed from one side, this circular motion appears as an oscillation back-and-forth and radiates an electromagnetic wave just as the oscillating current in a radio antenna does. For electrons moving at speeds very close to that of light, with resultant energies greater than $10^9$ eV, the photons produced in this way can be in the visual, ultraviolet, or even the X-ray range. The spectrum emitted is continuous. It is this process that produces the radio waves from extragalactic sources (such as quasars); the absorption of these waves by hydrogen atoms was discussed in chapter 2.

On the right-hand side of figure 3.1, heavy vertical lines indicate three regions of the spectrum in which new observational tools for interstellar matter research have become available, providing important new results in the decade 1970–80. The numbers indicate the order in which these three techniques are discussed in the following sections. The instrumental developments in the first two wavelength regions (the ultraviolet and the short-wavelength microwave) have opened essentially new areas of research. In the third wavelength region (X-rays), much active research was already underway before 1970; the instrumental development described at the end of this chapter is a satellite X-ray telescope, which was useful for one particularly important interstellar program. (The chief objectives of the fascinating overall X-ray program have been to investigate problems such as neutron stars, black holes, and clusters of galaxies, which are not directly related to the interstellar gas.)

Although not covered in this book, both gamma and infrared radiation can yield fundamental information on the interstellar medium. In particular, infrared photons escape without absorption from deep within interstellar clouds, where star formation is going on. As yet, most infrared measures have not had sufficient *spectral resolution*—that is, a sufficiently narrow measurement band—to separate out and identify the various atomic and molecular emission features. With the more powerful equipment now envisaged for future artificial satellites, the infrared should yield decisive results on various interstellar problems.

## ULTRAVIOLET SATELLITE TELESCOPES

The *Copernicus* satellite was planned mainly for research on the gas between the stars. More specifically, the 32-inch (80-cm) telescope and accompanying instrumentation for accurate measures of ultraviolet spectra that it carried aloft were designed to detect absorption of starlight by interstellar atoms and molecules. As indicated in table 3.1, most of these particles do not absorb visible light at all when they are in their ground states; the energy of a visual photon is insufficient to produce excitation from the ground state.

In fact interstellar atoms spend almost all their time in their ground states. This is because both the processes that excite particles—collisions with other particles and absorption of photons—are very infrequent in the dark, nearly empty space between the stars. Excitation of an atom to an excited state rarely occurs more than once a year. In marked contrast, the lifetime of most excited states, before a downward transition occurs spontaneously, is a small fraction of a microsecond. For example, if a group of hydrogen atoms are in the first excited orbit, half of them will move down to the ground orbit in $1.1 \times 10^{-9}$ sec. Evidently at any one time only a very small fraction of atoms will be in these excited states, and absorption of photons by such excited atoms is negligible. As we shall see in chapter 5, a similar conclusion holds for molecules also.

Since we have seen that most atoms and molecules in their ground states cannot absorb visible light, the concentration of interstellar particles in these states means that we cannot detect most of them from the ground. However, all these particles strongly absorb light waves in the ultraviolet, at wavelengths too short to permit passage through the atmosphere. It is such photons (with wavelength values, $\lambda$, between 920 and 3,000 Å) that *Copernicus* has detected, revolutionizing our knowledge of the material between the stars.

To show the usefulness of the ultraviolet in detecting many interstellar elements, we consider the absorption produced by the ten most abundant types of atoms, listed in table 1.1. Of these, only two, magnesium and iron, absorb visible light in their ground states, and only then, if they are in the form of neutral atoms. It happens that these two elements are ionized even more rapidly than sodium and calcium, which were discussed in the preceding chapter. As a result, neutral atoms of these elements are so rare in interstellar space that their absorption features are very weak and have been measured from the ground in only a few cases. With the Copernicus satellite, interstellar absorption features have been measured from all the elements in table 1.1 except helium and neon (the two inert gases), whose absorption occurs at wavelengths even shorter than 900 Å. Moreover, absorption features produced by interstellar atoms in various stages of ionization have also been measured, including silicon and sulphur, each with one, two, or three electrons removed, nitrogen missing four electrons ($N^{+4}$), and oxygen missing five ($O^{+5}$).

The situation with the next ten most abundant elements is somewhat similar. While eight of them have absorption features in visible light, most such features are produced by neutral atoms. Since the atoms of these elements are mostly ionized in interstellar space, measures of these visible features do not give very useful information on the abundance of the elements in question. (Except for sodium and potassium, most interstellar absorption features of these neutral atoms are usually too weak to measure in any case.) Observations at wavelengths between 900 and 3,000 Å can detect most of these elements in their most abundant ionization stages. A more detailed comparison of the elements observed from Copernicus and from the ground appears in chapter 6.

To tap this rich source of interstellar information in ultraviolet absorption features was the principal goal of the Copernicus instrument. Before discussing the characteristics of the spacecraft and the instrument itself, we list the three principal scientific requirements to be satisfied:

1. Ultraviolet sensitivity. The equipment should be able to detect ultraviolet radiation that cannot penetrate our atmosphere ($\lambda < 3,000$ Å). Sensitivity is particularly needed at wavelengths between 900 and 1,150 Å, to permit measures of some particularly important atoms and molecules between the stars (D, $H_2$, $N^+$, $O^{+5}$, etc.).

2. Spectral resolution. The measurement band of the spectrometer should be narrow enough to distinguish narrow inter-

stellar absorption features from wider, rotationally broadened stellar features. A band width of 0.05 Å at 1,000 Å permits resolution of two components of an absorption feature if their radial velocities differ by 15 km sec⁻¹.

3. Measurement accuracy. When the telescope is viewing a bright star, the equipment should be able to measure the profile of an absorption feature—the relative amount of energy at different wavelengths—with an error of less than one percent.

These requirements are easy to list, but to build an instrument that would satisfy them and a spacecraft to accommodate the instrument took more than a decade and many millions of dollars.

The development and launch of the Princeton telescope-spectrometer formed part of a general program of Orbiting Astronomical Observatories, organized by the National Aeronautics and Space Administration (NASA) in 1959–60, shortly after the agency was established in 1958. The NASA plan was to build (under supervision of the Goddard Space Flight Center) four identical spacecraft and to launch them with different astronomical instruments, each measuring ultraviolet starlight for a different scientific purpose. Each spacecraft was to contain engineering equipment for providing electrical power, receiving commands by radio, pointing the telescope, storing the scientific data, and then transmitting these data back to Earth by radio. In each, the astronomical instrumentation was to occupy an inner cylinder, some eight feet long and four feet in diameter, within the spacecraft.

According to the original NASA plan, the first spacecraft would carry the simplest instrument, and the Princeton telescope-spectrometer would be launched last, since it needed the most precise pointing. As it turned out, the first and third spacecrafts were unsuccessful: the first, launched in 1966, failed in orbit after a few days because of a failure in the power supply circuits; the third fell into the Indian Ocean during the attempted launch. The second and fourth spacecrafts were fully successful and obtained scientific data for many years.

The second Orbiting Astronomical Observatory, designated OAO-2, was designed to detect stars in ultraviolet light and to measure their spectra in the ultraviolet with a relatively wide measurement band (15 Å or more). Instrumentation for this purpose was provided by the University of Wisconsin and the Smithsonian Astrophysical Observatory. With such low spectral resolution, OAO-2 was not able to detect or measure most interstellar features, although measurements on the wide hydrogen absorption feature at 1216 Å and on ultraviolet absorption by dust provided important information for interstellar research.

We turn now to a detailed discussion of the instrumentation on the fourth orbiting Astronomical Observatory, *Copernicus*, including the principal components, their purpose and function, and how they performed in orbit. The arrangement of the main optical elements is shown in the cutaway drawing in figure 3.2. Light from a star travels down the telescope axis and strikes the 32-inch diameter primary mirror at the far end. The reflected light beam converges toward the convex secondary mirror at the front end of the telescope and after this second reflection converges more slowly to reach a focus about half way down the telescope, at the front end of the box containing the spectrometer. Here the starlight is focussed in a tiny image, which is supposed to be exactly on a very narrow slit, 24 microns (about one thousandth of an inch) in width. If the instrument is operating properly, half the starlight goes through the entrance slit into the spectrometer box.

The spectrometer is designed to spread the starlight into its component wavelengths and to measure the number of photons arriving within narrow wavelength bands. Light entering the spectrometer box through the entrance slit strikes a grating and is dispersed—that is, light of different wavelengths is sent off in different directions. The grating surface is concave, and each wavelength is focussed at some location on a circle one meter in diameter. Several photomultiplier tubes, or phototubes, can be positioned along an arc of this circle. A phototube has the convenient property that it will generate a short, intense pulse of electric current whenever an ultraviolet photon knocks a free electron out of the sensitive surface in the phototube (which it does only a few percent of the time). A narrow exit slit in front of the phototube ensures that at any one time this detector is sensitive only to the narrow range of wavelengths within the desired measurement band—0.05 Å at 1,000 Å. The starlight that strikes the side plates, or jaws, of the entrance slit is not wasted but is reflected off to one side and is used for guiding the telescope, to ensure that the stellar image stays centered on the slit so that the light passes into the spectrometer; a pointing stability better than 0.1 second of arc is required.

In operation, when the telescope is pointed at some bright star, each phototube sits quietly at one wavelength for 14 seconds. During this interval, electrical circuits count up the number of photon pulses produced by each phototube and at the end of the 14-second

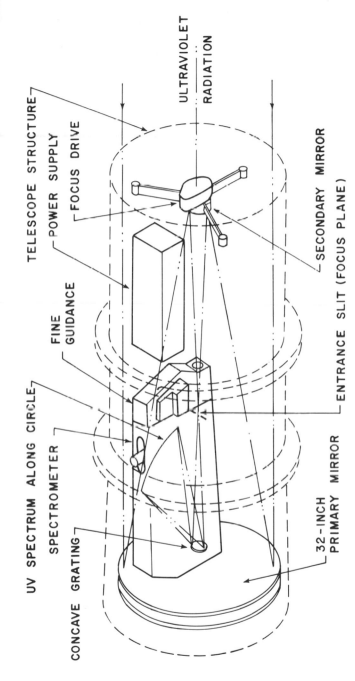

FIGURE 3.2 Diagram of the Copernicus telescope-spectrometer. The dashed lines show the telescope structure and the supporting rings; the solid lines, the telescope and its instrumentation; the dashed-dotted lines, the path followed by ultraviolet starlight.

counting interval store this number in the spacecraft memory. Then each phototube is moved to a slightly different position, and a new counting interval begins. A plot of these 14-second counts against the wavelength at which each count is obtained provides a precise measurement of the stellar spectrum, or at least a small part of it.

Once each orbit around the Earth (about every 100 minutes), the Orbiting Observatory establishes radio contact with one of several NASA ground stations, sends down all the scientific data obtained since the last radio contact, and receives any new commands needed for the next orbit. The data are transmitted by radio to the Goddard Space Flight Center (the NASA laboratory that operates most unmanned scientific satellites), and a day or so later are transmitted to Princeton for analysis and study by astronomers.

The photon counts studied by the astronomers do not give exactly the rate at which such photons reach the Earth. Because of light losses at reflecting surfaces and inefficiences in photon detection, only a small fraction of the photons entering the telescope in each wavelength band in a 14-second interval actually gets counted. Fortunately, we do not need to know the exact rate of photon arrival. It is the relative number that is required—the correct ratios of photons received at different wavelengths—and such ratios are given correctly.

While these functions are not very complicated in principle, designing, building, and testing the hardware required to perform them was a long and complex task. Princeton's contract with NASA for this enterprise began in 1962; some work on hardware design, first supported by the Air Force and then by NASA, had been in progress for three years before this. The final detailed design and fabrication were carried out for Princeton by the Sylvania Electronic Systems and Perkin Elmer Corporations, under subcontracts.

The successful performance both of the spacecraft and the telescope-spectrometer required the solution of many novel engineering problems. When this program began, space research was still in its infancy, and nothing very complicated had been launched. The objective was reliable operation of intricate electronic equipment for at least a year, with no possibility of any repairs, little possibility of a second try, and much money and scientific effort at stake. Since the chance of failure increases as a system becomes more complicated, the scientific functions of the instrument were kept very simple. In addition, redundant units were provided whenever possible to replace any that might fail.

Many engineering difficulties were created by the requirement for guidance stability within 0.1 second of arc. This tiny angle is the apparent separation between a man's eyes at a distance of about 150km! To maintain good optical alignment, the temperature of the instrument had to be kept nearly constant; to achieve this without adding regulatory thermostats and control circuits, which might themselves fail, posed many challenges. The problems involved in operating many of the components, especially the high-voltage equipment, in a high vacuum were perhaps the most serious of all; during its few days of operation, OAO-1 had encountered severe problems from high-voltage electric arcs. We devoted much effort to anticipating difficulties that might arise during high-vacuum orbital operation, when the equipment would also be subject to bombardment by energetic particles. The detailed tests of the instrument, especially in a vacuum, were of vital importance in revealing points where equipment failures might occur in the unfamiliar, and somewhat hostile, environment of outer space.

Difficulties also arose from the scientific requirement that the instrument operate effectively at wavelengths shorter than 1,150 Å. This forced us to use lithium fluoride coatings on the aluminum mirrors and photomultiplier tubes with no windows. Although a mirror coated with lithium fluoride reflects about 50 percent of the light at 1,025 Å, much more than any other surface, it deteriorates rapidly when exposed to air with appreciable humidity or other contaminants. Windowless photomultiplier tubes also degrade as a result of contamination and have the further disadvantage that they operate only in a vacuum. These complications created constant difficulties in the course of instrument assembly and testing, which went on for several years.

At one point, when the mirror surfaces had all degraded because of contamination, and several windowless photomultiplier tubes of novel design had failed in vacuum tests, we seriously considered replacing these unconventional techniques with more standard ones, which would have meant giving up wavelengths shorter than 1,150 Å. We finally decided to stick to the original goals: the photomultiplier tubes were repaired, and about seven months before the launch, the primary mirror and other optical elements were taken out, stripped, and recoated. It is very fortunate that we followed this route. Most of the Copernicus results reported in this book are based on results obtained at wavelengths shorter than 1,150 Å.

Tests and checks of the equipment continued up until a few hours before launching at Cape Kennedy, Florida. The problems and perils of these space programs are illustrated by our experience with the focus drive for the Princeton telescope. Focussing was provided by moving the secondary mirror back and forth along the axis; to do this, a special remote-control motor was provided. As a backup for the focus drive, we planned to place the secondary mirror in the best focal position before the launch. The instrument had been properly focussed on the ground months before the launch, and a correction had been made to take into account the absence of weight in orbit. A few hours before the launch I made a detailed check of all the instrument settings, and found to my alarm that an error had apparently been made in computing this correction. Urgent telephone calls to the various project engineers, mostly at Cape Kennedy for the launch, verified this conclusion. So just before the instrument was turned off in preparation for the launch, the operator at the console moved the secondary mirror to a new position. Several days after the launch, when our equipment was turned on, we were dismayed to discover that the focus motor failed to operate; presumably the intense vibration during launch had somehow damaged the motor or its electrical controls. To our intense relief, the telescope turned out to be in good focus anyway! Were it not for this last-minute correction, the usefulness of Copernicus would have been greatly reduced.

The launch into orbit on August 21, 1972, with an Atlas-Centaur rocket, went according to plan; the spacecraft was placed in a circular orbit about 750 kilometers above the Earth's surface. Figure 3.3 is a photograph of the launch, at about 5:30 a.m. After the launch the satellite was named Copernicus, in honor of the great Polish astronomer whose 500th birthday was being celebrated during 1972–73. An artist's sketch of Copernicus in orbit is shown in figure 3.4.

Apart from an unexpectedly high noise level in the phototubes used for wavelengths from 1,600 to 3,200 Å, wavelengths of secondary interest for interstellar studies, the performance of the equipment on Copernicus proved to be fully satisfactory. In particular, the three scientific requirements listed above were fully satisfied. Scans of various interstellar absorption features obtained with this instrument are shown in figure 3.5. In each plot, the observed 14-second counts have been divided by some power of 10, as indicated, and have been plotted against wavelength. The $N^+$ absorption feature is a blend of a wide component, produced in the atmosphere of Upsilon Scorpii (a bright star in the constellation Scorpius), and a narrow interstellar one. If the width of the measurement band were much greater than 0.05 Å, the separation of these two components would not be possible.

The Copernicus telescope-spectrometer continued to operate around the clock until February 15, 1981, when operations were ter-

FIGURE 3.3 Launch of the *Copernicus* satellite. The Atlas first-stage rocket has just started its long ascent from Cape Kennedy shortly before dawn on August 21, 1972. The Centaur second-stage rocket takes the observatory up to a circular orbit around the Earth at an altitude of about 750 km.

FIGURE 3.4 The *Copernicus* satellite in orbit about the Earth. The spacecraft is the octagonal structure, to which radio antennae and small, star-tracking telescopes are attached. The power cells, which generate electricity from sunlight, are attacked to the large planar arrays on each side. A light baffle extends in front to keep sunlight and earthlight out of the telescope aperture.

minated by NASA. During the last few years, the sensitivity of the instrument at wavelengths between 1,000 and 1,600 Å, the range of greatest usefulness for interstellar studies, seriously declined, presumably because of contamination of the mirrors and the photomultiplier tubes. As a result observations at the end were restricted to relatively bright stars. Throughout its life, the instrument was used not only by Princeton astronomers but also by visiting scientists from all over the world. About half the telescope time was allocated to these guest observers, who obtained data on stars, planets, comets, and the atmosphere of the Earth, in addition to the material between the stars. Some two hundred astronomers participated in these programs during *Copernicus's* 8-year operational life, the longest yet attained by any satellite used for observing the stars. Because of its

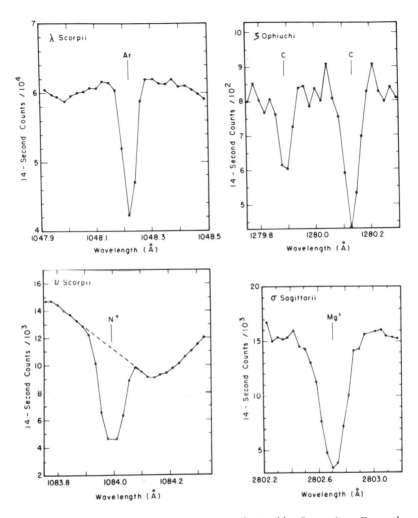

FIGURE 3.5 Representative spectrum scans obtained by *Copernicus*. For each absorption feature, the vertical line represents the central wavelength; the element producing the feature is also indicated. The dashed line indicates what the spectrum of Upsilon Scorpii looked like before any interstellar absorption.

great altitude, the Copernicus satellite is expected to stay in orbit, an inert, slowly tumbling hulk, for at least another century.

## DETECTORS FOR MICROWAVES

All radio waves are detected by means of the oscillating electrical currents to which they give rise. Except near a powerful transmitter, these waves are generally very weak, and the electrical currents that they produce in antennae are also weak. These currents must therefore be amplified before they can be detected and measured accurately. The amplification and final measurement are generally carried out with the aid of transistors and tuned electrical circuits.

Such techniques have been developed extensively for the waves of relatively long wavelength used in radio and television and have been much used by radio astronomers. Although, in principle, the same techniques can also be applied to microwaves, in practice, the high frequencies of microwaves create difficult problems. An electrical current, like a moving body, has an inertia of its own, and strong electrical forces are required if its direction is to be reversed very frequently. These difficulties become particularly serious if the frequency, $\nu$, is so high that the wavelength $(c/\nu)$ is less than the dimensions of the electrical circuit. When this happens, the time required for an electrical signal to travel across the circuit exceeds the period of a single oscillation, and different parts of the same circuit can behave in quite different ways. Thus to be useful, microwave circuits must be smaller than the wavelength of the radiation that they are to detect. For measuring the photons emitted by interstellar carbon monoxide molecules, which have a wavelength of 0.26 cm, this restriction is a serious one.

To make microwave detection practical, the incoming signal is converted as quickly as possible into an alternating electrical current at a much lower frequency, which can then be amplified and measured with electrical circuits of a more convenient size. This objective is achieved using a superheterodyne technique. To follow recent advances in microwave technology, it is necessary to have some understanding of this technique.

In the superheterodyne approach, the incoming radio signal of frequency $\nu$ is combined with the signal from a local oscillator. This oscillator, which can form an integral part of the receiver, has a frequency slightly different from $\nu$. These two signals are shown, each plotted against time, in diagram A of figure 3.6; the two curves, which for simplicity are assumed to have the same amplitude, are superposed on each other. The sum of the two signals, plotted again

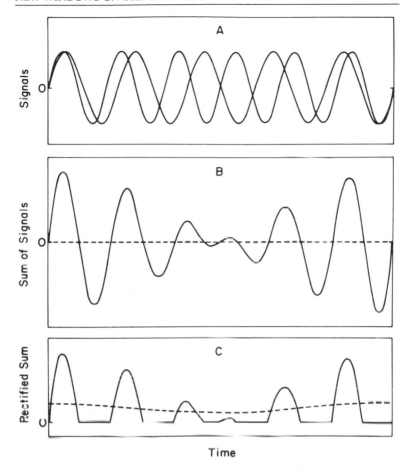

Time

FIGURE 3.6 Principle of superheterodyne technique. In diagram A two separate oscillating signals are shown, each plotted against time. Their frequencies
differ slightly. Diagram B shows their sum. Diagram C shows the signal obtained by passing the summed signal in B through a rectifier. The dashed line
shows the resulting oscillation at the beat frequency, together with an average,
steady (DC) current.

against time, is shown in diagram B. What is essentially happening
here is that the signal with the higher frequency continually gains on
the other. If the oscillations are initially in phase, they will add at
the beginning to give an increased signal. Some time later they are
out of phase and oppose each other, reducing the net signal.

Diagram C shows what happens if the output signal from B is put through a rectifier, which passes current in one direction only. As shown by the dashed line, there is an average direct current and an oscillation at a lower frequency, sometimes called the *beat* frequency. In diagram B the corresponding low-frequency components are zero. If the rectified signal is passed into a receiver tuned to the beat frequency, it is then possible to obtain amplification and detection at this lower or intermediate, frequency.

In practice the current produced by the original radio signal is generally much weaker than the current from the local oscillator. In addition, the two currents are generally combined in a *mixer*, which need not fully rectify the total current. However, the final effect is still the production of an oscillating intermediate signal at the beat frequency.

The superheterodyne technique was originally designed for standard radio sets to avoid the inconvenience of having to tune each of the circuits that successively amplified the radio signal. If the intermediate frequency is kept constant, only the local oscillator needs to be tuned.

For microwave reception the superheterodyne approach is vital, since it permits the required use of lower frequencies for amplification. With this approach only two elements must operate at a very high frequency—the local oscillator and the mixer. Continual progress has been made in pushing these devices to higher and higher frequencies. Special tubes called *klystrons* have been developed which produce radio oscillations at frequencies as high as 150 GHz ($150 \times 10^9$ Hz). This successful technique involves oscillating clouds of electrons, thereby avoiding any high-frequency currents in wires. To obtain a mixer that would operate at such a high frequency, a special diode was constructed at the Bell Telephone Laboratories, using a tiny gold dot, about 2 microns ($2 \times 10^{-4}$ cm) in diameter, electroplated on a small chip of a semiconducting material a few hundredths of a centimeter across, fastened to a conductor.

This exceedingly tiny diode carries current in one direction only, so in this case the mixer is actually a rectifier. A short spring, whose tip is placed against the dot, serves as an antenna and produces electrical current in response to the two passing waves, that of the radio signal and that produced by the local oscillator. The current of very high frequency is evidently limited to the regions of the spring and the diode that make up the mixer-rectifier. The current passing through the diode and on into the conductor is already rectified, and its important oscillation is at the intermediate frequency. In the device used to detect radiation emitted by the astrophysically important interstellar carbon monoxide molecule, at 0.26 cm wavelength, the intermediate frequency was about 1.4 GHz, much less than the 115 GHz of the carbon monoxide radiation itself. The sharpness of tuning of the intermediate-frequency circuit determines the width of the measurement band for the incoming radio waves. The first measurements of interstellar carbon monoxide made with this equipment were reported in 1970. In the ensuing decade a new field of interstellar research in microwave molecular spectroscopy blossomed, and emission features were subsequently measured at wavelengths as short as 0.1 cm.

## X-RAY MEASURES FROM SATELLITES

X-ray photons, like ultraviolet photons, are strongly absorbed by the Earth's atmosphere. Thus research in both of these regions of the electromagnetic spectrum requires space vehicles. However, for interstellar investigations, these two research areas differ significantly in their requirements. Progress in interstellar studies with ultraviolet light requires the measurement of narrow absorption features in stellar spectra. This objective requires a large, accurately pointed space telescope, such as Copernicus. X-ray photons are produced by emission from supernova remnants and from hot gas elsewhere in the Galaxy. To investigate such emission, at least in a preliminary fashion, requires neither very precise pointing nor a very narrow measurement band. Toward the end of chapter 2 we saw that substantial progress was made in interstellar X-ray research in the 1970s with the use of relatively small sounding rockets, which carried instruments into space for a few minutes.

Even with a relatively modest instrument, a place in a scientific satellite in orbit around the Earth offers the great advantage of a long observing time, much more than can be obtained in a few sounding-rocket flights. During the decade 1970–80, soft X-rays, which are of particular interstellar interest, were observed from several satellites. One representative of this group made use of the Skylab program.

Skylab was a very large scientific satellite, which was designed for many months of operation with several shifts of astronauts. It was constructed from parts developed for the Apollo Moon landings and included a large module with laboratory and living space for the astronauts. Many different instruments were flown on this satellite, including a telescope for research on the Sun. Several other large satellites, used to ferry the astronaut crews from Earth up into space, accompanied Skylab during a few of its many orbits around the

Earth. Launched in 1973, Skylab was operated at intervals during a nine-month period and was then abandoned. It fell down to Earth in 1979, with assorted parts reaching the ground along a path across Australia.

One of the instruments associated with Skylab was a detector for soft X-rays with energies less than about 280 eV (wavelengths longer than 44 Å). This instrument was placed in one of the accompanying satellites, where it operated unattended during its several hours in orbit. In chapter 2 we noted that soft X-rays reach the Earth from all over the sky, with greatest intensity in regions well away from the Milky Way (that is, in high galactic latitudes). Possible theoretical origins were either emission from many stars or emission from a hot ionized interstellar gas at a temperature of about a million degrees Kelvin. The soft X-ray detector associated with Skylab was designed by a group at the University of Wisconsin to search for such photons from known stars, to provide a test for the stellar origin theory. No soft X-rays were observed from any known stars or in fact from any pointlike sources.

Similar results were obtained during this decade not only from sounding-rocket flights, but also from a small telescope for soft X-rays provided for the *Copernicus* satellite by a group at University College, London. The latter instrument was included in *Copernicus* by NASA so that if the ultraviolet telescope failed to perform properly, the satellite would still have a useful scientific function. About a tenth of the total satellite observing time was allocated to this X-ray instrument. Observations of several bright stars with this instrument failed to show any measurable soft X-ray emission. (Observations with much more sensitive equipment a number of years later have shown that soft X-rays are in fact emitted by many stars but are too weak to account for the general background of soft X-rays.) As we shall see in chapter 6, this X-ray evidence supports the *Copernicus* ultraviolet data in the discovery of a hot interstellar gas.

## SUMMARY

The study of interstellar matter has been profoundly influenced by new developments in instrumentation during the decade 1970–80. Three of these new tools were designed to extend astronomical observations into regions of the electromagnetic spectrum not previously explored in any detail.

The *Copernicus* satellite carried a telescope-spectrometer designed to measure ultraviolet stellar spectra with high resolution.

The chief purpose of this instrument was to measure the absorption features produced by atoms and molecules between the stars. Most such particles absorb only in the ultraviolet and therefore cannot be detected in visible light. The telescope, with its 32-inch–diameter mirror and its high-resolution spectrometer, which used a concave grating to disperse the light into its component wavelengths and several phototubes to detect individual photons at each wavelength, operated satisfactorily for some eight years. The guidance system kept the telescope pointed at a star to within less than 0.1 second of arc. The measuring band width at 1,000 Å was 0.05 Å, permitting very precise measures of narrow absorption features. The equipment was used by several hundred astronomers, not only for pioneering interstellar studies, but for other astronomical research programs as well.

New detectors developed by radio astronomers made it possible to extend radio observations down to wavelengths as short as 0.26 cm, the wavelength of the strong emission from the carbon monoxide molecule. This molecule, one of the most abundant in interstellar clouds, cannot be observed in visible light. Extensive observations of interstellar carbon monoxide have been made with such detectors.

Measurement of soft X-rays from the sky, at energies between 250 and 1,000 eV, was greatly aided by the availability of satellites as platforms for this instrumentation. A satellite launched in connection with the Skylab program was successfully used for soft X-ray observations and took the lead in showing that the general background of radiation observed at energies less than 280 eV was not emitted by known stars.

# 4

# Primordial Hydrogen in the Galactic Disc

The gas between the stars, like that in the stars themselves, is mostly hydrogen, the lightest element. Helium atoms are also present, with one such atom for every ten of hydrogen. These atoms are primordial, in that they were produced in the initial Big Bang. Atoms of various heavier elements, which have been produced more recently, are present only as slight impurities. By normal standards, the gas between the stars would pass as a pure hydrogen-helium mixture.

Measures with *Copernicus* can determine accurately the amount of this primordial hydrogen along the line of sight between the Earth and a hot star. Specifically, measures of a hydrogen absorption feature in the spectrum of a hot star can be used to evaluate the column density of neutral hydrogen atoms along the line of sight. This column density, $N(H)$, was defined earlier as the number of hydrogen atoms in a long, thin cylinder, 1 $cm^2$ in cross-section, extending along the line of sight. In the discussion of absorption features, the line of sight stops at the star whose light is being absorbed. For a star some thousand light years distant, numerical values of $N(H)$ are usually between $10^{19}$ and $10^{21}$ $cm^{-2}$—very large numbers, which correspond to very little mass, however, at most about 0.001 gm $cm^{-2}$.

These values of $N(H)$ along the lines of sight to different stars can enhance our knowledge of the interstellar medium in three ways. First, the numerical results can be compared with similar results for dust grains, and the ratio of gas to dust can be determined. Astronomers have argued for decades over whether or not a cloud of dust is also a cloud of gas—a question of some importance for cloud evolution and star formation.

Second, a value of $N(H)$ toward a star can be divided by the known distance, $L$, of the star to give $n(H)$, the average particle density of neutral hydrogen atoms between the Earth and the star. In this way, average hydrogen densities in different directions and at different distances from the Sun can be found.

Third, measurement of similar absorption features for deuterium, the heavy isotope of hydrogen, can evaluate the ratio of deuterium to hydrogen in the interstellar gas. The theory of deuterium formation during the Big Bang then gives a clue as to the present density of the Universe.

These topics are discussed in detail in this chapter. The initial section describes how observations of absorption features in general can be used to determine the column densities of the absorbing atoms. This is basic for the *Copernicus* results presented in the subsequent sections.

## EVALUATION OF COLUMN DENSITIES

One of the most evident characteristics of science is its reliance on numbers. To verify or refute a theory requires a comparison between numbers obtained from observations and numbers computed from the theory. In the previous chapter, we saw how the *Copernicus* instrumentation gives definite numbers for the interstellar absorption features in the spectra of hot stars. In particular, a typical scan gives the number of photons counted during 14 seconds at each of several wavelengths spread across a feature. In the present section we see how these 14 second counts can be used to determine the column densities of absorbing atoms. Fortunately it is possible to describe the principles involved in this process without going through the mathematical equations involved.

The first step is to express the observational results in the best form for showing the amount of interstellar absorption. For this purpose we are interested in the fraction of the starlight that has been absorbed at each wavelength. Thus to measure the absorption, we should divide the photon count at a particular wavelength by what the count would have been if no absorption feature had been present; this latter count represents the intrinsic spectrum of the star, which we shall refer to as the *source spectrum*. Of course, we cannot measure the source spectrum directly, but as we saw in chapter 2, if the star used as a light source is rotating rapidly, all of its intrinsic absorption features are broadened by about an Ångstrom and can readily be distinguished from the interstellar features, most of which are relatively narrow, as shown in figure 3.5. Thus the $N^+$ feature shown in this figure can easily be distinguished from the broader absorption feature produced by ionized nitrogen atoms in the source star, Upsilon Scorpii.

Figure 4.1 shows how the observational data for the absorption feature produced by interstellar $N^+$ are presented so as to indicate numerically the amount of interstellar atomic absorption. In this figure the data are replotted to show values of the relative intensity, r, which was introduced earlier in connection with the absorption feature profiles shown in figures 2.3 and 2.5. To obtain these values of r, the 14-second count at each wavelength is divided by the corresponding count at the same wavelength in the source spectrum, shown by the dashed line in figure 3.5. (The effect of stray light in

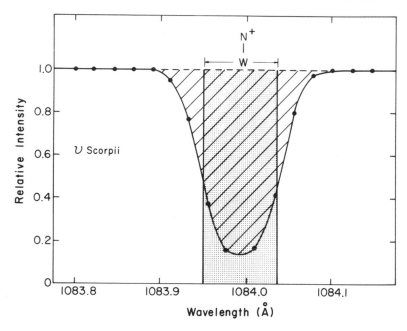

FIGURE 4.1 Absorption feature of interstellar $N^+$. The observed spectrum of Upsilon Scorpii, in the vicinity of the $N^+$ absorption shown in figure 3.5, has been divided by the assumed source spectrum (dashed line in figure 3.5) to give values of the relative intensity, r, for the interstellar feature. The strength of this feature is measured by the absorbed area, W (measured in Å), of the diagonally hatched region. To help visualize the significance of the absorbed area, the shaded rectangle shows an idealized absorption feature with zero central intensity and width W; the area of this rectangle equals the area of the actual absorption feature.

the spectrograph, which increases the 14-second counts by the same amount at all wavelengths near the absorption feature, has also been corrected for.) The depth of the absorption feature is found by subtracting the relative intensity from 1. Thus, if the relative intensity has the high value of 0.9, for example, the depth will be small, equalling 0.1. As the relative intensity falls to zero, the depth rises to 1.

The area of the diagonally hatched region in figure 4.1 we call the *absorbed area* of the absorption feature and denote by $W$. This region is bounded below by the curve for the observed relative intensity and above by the dashed horizontal line representing no interstellar absorption. The horizontal scale in the figure is in units of wavelength, whereas the vertical scale is dimensionless. Hence the absorbed area is given in units of wavelength, and we express $W$ in Ångstroms. (For the $N^+$ absorption feature shown, $W = 0.086$ Å.)

It may be helpful to think of $W$ as the width of the shaded rectangle in figure 4.1. This rectangle is drawn to have the same area as the diagonally hatched region; since its height equals 1, its width must equal $W$. (Astronomers generally call $W$ the *equivalent width* of an absorption feature.) The Copernicus instrument has been used to determine values of $W$ in a wide variety of absorption features.

We may note in passing that the absorption by dust, which is reasonably constant over many Ångstroms, is not detected by this procedure. Thus, what we have called the source spectrum is really the source spectrum as modified by dust absorption. This is all quite satisfactory, since we are not interested here in the source spectrum for its own sake. Our goal is to measure the absorption provided in some particular feature by atoms or molecules.

Because the absorbed area, $W$, is related to the column density of absorbing atoms, $N$, the values of $W$ found from this procedure give values for $N$. There is a relationship between $W$ and $N$, which can be used to determine the second quantity from the first. A plot of the relationship between $W$ and $N$ is called a *curve of growth*, since it shows how an absorption feature grows as the number of absorbing atoms increases.

To illustrate the nature of such a curve we consider an idealized absorption feature produced by atoms whose velocities of recession or approach (radial velocities) extend over a range of 25 km sec$^{-1}$. For an absorption feature at 1,200 Å, the Doppler effect (see p. 30) caused by these atomic motions gives a total width of 0.10 Å. We denote this width by the symbol $w$. If we assume that all velocities within this range are equally likely, then the absorption produced in this feature will be the same at all wavelengths within this range and zero outside. Plots of the resultant absorption feature are shown in the upper diagram of figure 4.2. The uppermost profile in this diagram, with a relative intensity of 0.90, is computed for a reasonably typical absorption feature with a column density of $10^{13}$ $cm^{-2}$. The other profiles, which have lower relative intensities (greater depths), are obtained when the column density is successively

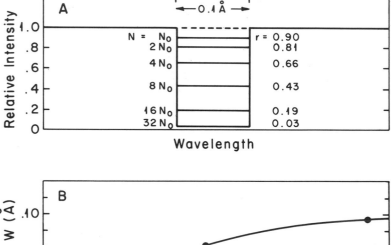

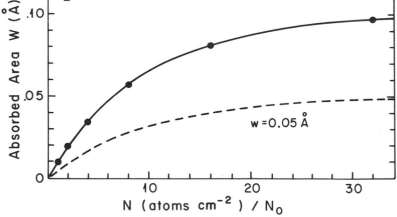

FIGURE 4.2 Idealized curve of growth. Diagram A shows the relative intensity, r, in idealized absorption features, each with a rectangular profile 0.10 Å wide, with the column density, N, successively multiplied by 2; the initial value of N, for which r = 0.9, is designated by $N_0$. Diagram B shows the curve of growth resulting when values of W, the absorbed area for each profile in diagram A, are plotted against $N/N_0$. For the dashed curve of growth in diagram B, the width, w, of the rectangular profile is reduced to 0.05 Å.

doubled, first to $2 \times 10^{13}$ cm$^{-2}$, then to $4 \times 10^{13}$ cm$^{-2}$, and so on, up to $32 \times 10^{13}$ cm$^{-2}$.

The rectangular profile shown for each of these absorption features is certainly idealized, but this simplified case is easy to understand. Such idealizations are frequently helpful to the theorist in preliminary thinking about a problem.

The lower diagram, B, in figure 4.2 shows a curve of growth obtained from the features in the upper diagram. It is of interest to examine why this curve has the shape indicated—that is, to show how the relative intensity, r, and the absorbed area, W, change each time N is doubled. For the lowest value of N, which we denote by $N_0$, the relative intensity is 0.90; that is, $9/10$ of the photons get through. When N is doubled, it is as though a second absorbing cloud, identical with the first, is placed in the line of sight. If $9/10$ of the photons get through the first cloud, $9/10$ of these transmitted photons will then get through the second cloud. It follows that the fraction of photons that pass through both clouds without absorption amounts to $9/10 \times 9/10$, or $81/100$. Thus, whenever N is doubled, the relative intensity, r, is squared. Hence, as N increases by successive powers of 2, the successive values of r are 0.9, 0.81, 0.66, 0.43, 0.19, and 0.03. For these idealized rectangular profiles, the absorbed area, W, equals the depth times w, the width. Since w is taken here to be constant at 0.10 Å for all values of N, and since the depth equals 1.0 minus the relative intensity, r, W increases from 0.010 up to 0.097 Å as N increases.

(These results may be summarized in a few simple equations. The relative intensity, r, may be expressed as

$$r = (0.90)^{N/N_0} = e^{-0.1 \, N/N_0}$$

and consequently the absorbed area is given by

$$W = w(1 - r) = w(1 - e^{-0.1 \, N/N_0}),$$

where e is the base of Napierian logarithms, and $\log_e 0.9 \approx -0.1$.)

The numerical results obtained above are shown by the data points on the solid curve in figure 4.2, diagram B. The dashed line shows the curve of growth obtained if the total width, w, in diagram A is reduced by one half to 0.05 Å. In both cases, as N increases, W approaches w as a limiting value.

Two parts of each curve of growth may be distinguished. When W is appreciably less than its limiting value, corresponding to depths less than about 0.2, the absorbed area varies almost in direct proportion to N. We shall call this the proportional section of the curve of growth. For absorption features that are weak enough to be on this proportional section, an accurate measurement of W determines N with about equal accuracy. In this section of the curve, $W$ depends very little on the line width, $w$, which therefore need not be known precisely for a good determination of $N$. Another advantage of the proportional section is that high spectroscopic resolution is not required to obtain useful results for absorption features on this section. The true profile of the absorption feature may show many components, each produced by a single cloud with its own Doppler shift, as shown by the interstellar data in figure 2.5. Even if the wavelength width of the measurement band in the spectrograph is relatively large, so that different components are blurred and appear as a single wide feature, the same proportional relationship between $W$ and $N$ is still valid, provided each component is relatively weak (that is, has a small depth).

The second part of the curve of growth is the flat section, where $W$ is close to its limiting value and scarcely varies at all with varying $N$. In this region of the curve, the relative intensity in the absorption feature is very small, and the depth is almost 1.0. The value of $W$ now gives information on the line width, $w$, but very little precise information on $N$. Lines in this region are said to be *saturated*; the depth of the feature and the absorbed area, $W$, have reached their maximum values, and $N$ can increase very substantially without an appreciable effect on $W$.

When actual profiles of absorption features are considered, the curves of growth are usually not much different from the idealized versions in figure 4.2. As already pointed out, the proportional section is not modified at all, even if the true line profile is very complex. The flat section is usually not completely horizontal but slopes slightly upward; that is, with increasing $N$, $W$ increases somewhat, but very slowly. For all practical purposes this section may still be regarded as flat. The transition region between the proportional and flat sections may become widened under some conditions, extending over a broader range of column densities. The two general conclusions remain: (a) weak lines are on the proportional, or unsaturated, section of the curve of growth, where $N$ may be found directly from $W$; (b) strong lines tend to be saturated, and only a lower limit for $N$ can be determined.

In this chapter and the two following chapters, extensive use is made of curves of growth in determinations of abundance of different species from the *Copernicus* data. These determinations are largely based on weak, unsaturated features. The high spectral resolution and high measurement accuracy of *Copernicus* are needed for accurate data on these weak features.

We turn now to the consideration of an important effect, ignored above, that permits an accurate determination of N (again the column density of the absorbing atoms) for the very strongest absorption features. The preceding discussion of the curve of growth assumes that if an atom is motionless and there is no Doppler shift, the atom will absorb at only one wavelength. This is almost true but not quite. As we saw at the beginning of chapter 2, an atom can absorb very weakly a photon whose wavelength, $\lambda$, is appreciably different from $\lambda_0$, the central wavelength of the absorption feature. If $\lambda$ differs from $\lambda_0$ by more than about 0.01 Å (but by much less than $\lambda_0$), the absorbing power of all the atoms present is proportional to $N/(\lambda-\lambda_0)^2$. For most interstellar atoms, this absorption is too weak to notice. However, for hydrogen, either atomic or molecular, the value of N is often so enormous that this absorption can be seen at wavelengths several Ångstroms away from $\lambda_0$. An absorption feature that is broadened in this way is said to possess wings.

Figure 4.3 shows a computed profile for the strongest absorption feature of atomic hydrogen, produced by a transition from the ground state to the first excited orbit. The center of this strong feature is at a wavelength of 1,215.7 Å. The strong absorption wings are evident. The particle column density, N(H), assumed here is $10^{20}$ cm$^{-2}$, enormously greater than the column densities of absorbing atoms in figure 4.2. A prominent characteristic of features with absorption wings is their great extent, particularly the very gradual disappearance of the absorption as $\lambda$ departs further and further from $\lambda_0$. At

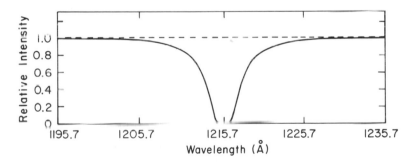

FIGURE 4.3 Profile of winged hydrogen feature. The solid line shows the relative intensity near the 1,216-Å hydrogen absorption feature for a source shining through a cloud with a hydrogen atom column density, N(H), equal to $10^{20}$ cm$^{-2}$. The intensity is shown relative to the source spectrum (indicated by the dashed line) in the absence of hydrogen absorption.

wavelengths such that the depth of the profile is small (less than about 0.2, for example), the depth is proportional to $N/(\lambda-\lambda_0)^2$. (The constant of proportionality here involves mostly the same atomic constants as are needed to compute the relation between $W$ and $N$ in the proportional section of the curve of growth.)

As shown by a comparison of figures 3.5 and 4.3, the weaker absorption features with no wings resemble more nearly the rectangular profiles of figure 4.2 than the winged profile of figure 4.3. Features without wings generally show relatively steep sides—that is, the depth goes to zero rather abruptly with increasing distance from the central wavelength.

Absorption features strong enough to show wings offer the attractive advantage that they yield accurate values of the column density, $N$. Although the center of such a feature is saturated, the wings are not; thus the depth in the wings is proportional to $N$. The distribution of particle velocities, which is usually not well known, has no effect on the wings. Furthermore, the measurement band of the Copernicus spectrometer is narrow enough to give the true profile of the wings. It would be possible to measure the absorbed area, $W$, for such a strong feature, and to include the effect of wings on the curve of growth. However, it is much more accurate to fit a theoretical profile to these observed wings, a process that determines $N$ rather precisely. In this way it has been possible to determine accurate values of $N(H)$ and also of $N(H_2)$, the corresponding particle density for molecular hydrogen. Copernicus observations have been used to obtain such values for the lines of sight to many stars. Wings may be marginally present for the strongest lines of the most abundant heavy atoms—carbon, nitrogen, and oxygen—but are so weak that they have seldom been used for determining column densities.

## CORRELATION OF GAS AND DUST

There has been a long-standing controversy over whether a cloud of dust is necessarily a cloud of gas, or whether two separate types of clouds exist, one composed of dust, the other of gas. To settle the argument one way or another requires measuring the amounts of gas and dust along a large number of lines of sight and examining the correlation.

The total number of hydrogen atoms along the line of sight to a hot star, including hydrogen atoms bound in $H_2$ molecules as well as free atoms, equals $N(H) + 2N(H_2)$; we denote this total hydrogen column density by $N(H_{Tot})$. The atomic and molecular hydrogen column densities, $N(H)$ and $N(H_2)$, must be evaluated separately. The values of $N(H)$ along the lines of sight to many hot stars have been determined from the wings of the very strong 1,216-Å feature discussed above. For this determination the 0.05-Å measurement band used for most interstellar studies with *Copernicus* is narrower than necessary. Since this strong hydrogen feature may be some 10 to 20 Å wide, it takes rather a long time to scan the entire feature with such a narrow band, with 14 seconds of photon counting at each wavelength. Instead, another *Copernicus* phototube with a wider measurement band—about 0.2 Å—has often been used. With four positions scanned per minute, in half an hour this lower-resolution phototube scans 24 Å and gives an accurate profile of the entire 1,216-Å feature in the spectrum of the star.

Most stellar atmospheres contain some atomic hydrogen, which produces wide absorption features in some stellar spectra. To be sure that we are looking at truly interstellar hydrogen absorption, we must view a light source in which neutral hydrogen is so scarce that it can be neglected in the source spectrum. Fortunately, stars whose surface temperature exceeds 20,000° K satisfy this requirement since hydrogen atoms in the atmospheres of such stars are mostly ionized and do not absorb light. Hence these hot stars have been used as light sources for detecting and measuring interstellar hydrogen atoms.

The column density, $N(H_2)$, for molecular hydrogen in these hot stars is found from the wings of the strong $H_2$ absorption features, which are discussed in the next chapter. A group of three such features at about 1,093 Å is usually used. Since there are virtually no $H_2$ molecules in a hot stellar atmosphere, there are no stellar $H_2$ absorption features to confuse with the interstellar ones.

For most hot stars in which $N(H_{Tot})$ has been measured with *Copernicus*, the column density of interstellar dust has been determined from telescopes on the ground. As pointed out in chapter 2, a dust grain absorbs blue light, with a relatively short wavelength, more strongly than red light, with a longer wavelength, exceeding the dimensions of the grain. As a result, stars seen through a cloud of dust appear reddened; that is, the radiant energy reaching the Earth at longer wavelengths is relatively greater than would be expected. Detailed measures of this reddening can be used to give values of the column density of the small solid particles along the line of sight to the star. (These computed column densities depend on the size and composition of the grains, but fortunately, different plausible assumptions give about the same results for the mass column density in gm cm$^{-2}$.)

Figure 4.4 shows a plot of $N(H_{Tot})$ against $N(grains)$ (with the latter expressed in terms of the reddening, or *color excess*). To obtain the exact total number of hydrogen nuclei present, allowance must be made for the presence of hydrogen in other forms besides neutral atoms and $H_2$ molecules. The largest term that should be added to $N(H_{Tot})$ is $N(H^+)$, or $N(p)$, the column density of ionized hydrogen at-

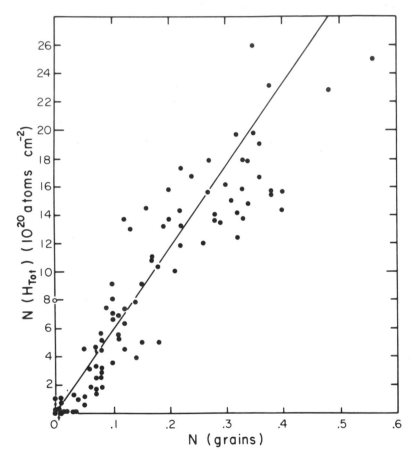

FIGURE 4.4 Column densities of gas and dust. The column density of hydrogen atoms, including both free neutral atoms and those bound up in hydrogen molecules, is plotted against the total amount of dust (as measured by the reddening) along the line of sight. Two points with arrows represent upper limits. The solid line shows a reasonable fit to the data.

oms, or protons; addition of this term, whose value is uncertain, might increase $N(H_{Tot})$ by some 10 percent.

It is evident from this figure that there is a strong correlation between $N(H_{Tot})$ and N(grains), although the correlation does not appear to be exact. To some extent the scatter of points from the straight line is due to errors in determining the two quantities, especially in the assumed properties of the intrinsic stellar spectra used to determine N(grains). Probably some of the scatter shown in figure 4.4 is real, though for most stars the gas-to-dust ratio, measured by $N(H_2)/$N(grains), is probably well within a factor of two of its average value. (For the discrepant star Rho Ophiuchi, for which the point falls off the figure, the gas-to-dust ratio is apparently some three times its average.)

Some astronomers have suggested that a correlation of the sort shown in figure 4.4 might result from the individual correlations of $N(H_{Tot})$ and N(grains) with distance along the line of sight. A detailed examination of the observations disproves this suggestion, however. Because of the patchy distribution of clouds, $N(H_{Tot})$ and N(grains) each show a poor correlation with the distance of the source star. As we saw in chapter 2, some relatively close stars, a few hundred light years away, happen to lie behind obscuring dust clouds and show strong reddening. A few very distant stars, several thousand light years away, on the other hand, show no appreciable reddening. In all these cases, $N(H_{tot})/$N(grains) remains about the same, and we conclude that the gas-to-dust ratio is roughly constant in most interstellar clouds. While some theorists had predicted this result, others had predicted just the opposite.

Indeed, there are a number of theoretical arguments indicating that the gas-to-dust ratio should have somewhat different values in different interstellar regions. If solid particles condense from the gas only in the extended atmospheres of stars, as suggested by some theorists, imperfect mixing might lead to variations in this ratio. Furthermore, even if this ratio were constant at one time, different forces acting on atoms and grains might separate one type of particle from the other, again producing variations in the ratio. Finally, in clouds moving at high velocities, the dust particles tend to evaporate (see chapter 6), and the gas-to-dust ratio must be markedly increased; such clouds are rare, however. While some such variations must be present in certain clouds, figure 4.4 indicates that along most lines of sight, these differences in the gas-to-dust ratio are not large.

The detailed correlation shown in figure 4.4 may be used to determine the amount of hydrogen in a typical clump of dust (see chapter 2). The resultant overall hydrogen column density, $N(H_{Tot})$, obtained in this way is $4 \times 10^{20}$ cm$^{-2}$. This value is in reasonably close agreement with that obtained from 21-cm absorption studies—namely, that $N(H)$ in diffuse clouds averages about $3 \times 10^{20}$ cm$^{-2}$. When the latter value is increased to allow for some molecular hydrogen also, these two results come into even closer agreement, providing further confirmation that a cloud of gas is indeed a cloud of dust as well. As in chapter 2, we refer to these clouds seen in absorption, produced by either hydrogen atoms or dust grains, as diffuse clouds.

One may wonder why the close relationship between dust and gas in the interstellar medium was not established earlier by observations with the 21-cm emission feature of neutral hydrogen. The primary difficulty with such an attempt is that the observed 21-cm emission feature in the direction of any particular star may come from anywhere along the line of sight, including regions of hydrogen much further away than the star. Clearly any dust grains associated with this more distant hydrogen will not produce any reddening of the star and will not be included in the value of $N(grains)$ found from the observed reddening. A secondary difficulty is that emission features, like absorption features, can also become saturated if $N$, the column density of emitting atoms, is sufficiently high. When this happens, $N$ can be much increased with relatively little change in the intensity of the observed emission. For some clouds, this effect can be significant for 21-cm radiation. Thus the true value of $N(H)$ between us and a star may be much less or much greater than the value found from 21-cm emission in the direction of the star. Results obtained from the 1,216-Å absorption feature are free of these difficulties and have therefore been of decisive importance.

## HYDROGEN PARTICLE DENSITY

As we have seen, the particle column density, $N(H)$, is the number of neutral hydrogen atoms per square centimeter along the line of sight to a star. As in chapter 2, we divide $N(H)$ by the stellar distance, $L$, (in cm) to determine the average particle density, $n(H)$, expressed as the number of neutral hydrogen atoms per cubic centimeter. (The distance, $L$, is again found from the measured star brightness, as on p. 43.) Thus Copernicus data give average values of $n(H)$ along the lines of sight to a wide variety of stars.

Because of the patchy distribution of interstellar matter, the values of $n(H)$ determined in this way are very different for different stars. The lowest observed values are about $10^{-2}$ cm$^{-3}$; the highest about 10 cm$^{-3}$, a range of more than a thousand. If an average is taken over all stars in the galactic disc within 3,000 light years of the Sun, we find that $n(H_{Tot})$ (including $H_2$) is 1.2 cm$^{-3}$, which is not inconsistent with the range of values found from the more approximate 21-cm emission data. If the gas within each star of the Galaxy were spread out uniformly over distances of a hundred or so light years, the contribution of known stars to $n(H_{Tot})$ in the galactic plane near the Sun would be 1.7 hydrogen atoms cm$^{-3}$. Within this region of the Galaxy, the mass of material between the stars is evidently about two-thirds of that in the known stars—a more precise form of the general result stated at the beginning of chapter 1.

Close to the Sun, the gas density is usually smaller. The general average of $n(H)$ for the lines of sight to stars within 300 light years is about 0.1 cm$^{-3}$. The value of $n(H)$ has also been determined for four stars within 15 light years of the Sun. These four very close objects are not hot stars, which provide ideal ultraviolet light sources, but cool stars, whose source spectra show a broad hydrogen emission feature at 1,216 Å. At the center of this feature, a narrow absorption feature appears, corresponding again to $n(H)$ equal to about 0.1 cm$^{-3}$. The occurrence of a cold diffuse cloud along the line of sight to such close stars is improbable, and the observed low-density gas may be regarded as intercloud material.

This low value of $n(H)$ near the Sun is confirmed by measures of the gas entering the solar system and sweeping by the Sun. The atoms of hydrogen and helium in this gas can be detected from the sunlight that they absorb and reemit at 1,216 and 584 Å, respectively. The particle density obtained in this way is again about 0.1 cm$^{-3}$ for hydrogen and one-tenth of this for helium. The gas temperature, which can also be found from such measures, is in the neighborhood of 10,000° K. Thus the Sun is definitely not in a typical diffuse cloud, in which $n(H)$ exceeds 10 cm$^{-3}$ and $T$ equals roughly 80° K, as we shall see in the next chapter. Instead, the temperature, and perhaps also the density, is characteristic of the warm gas that was found to be rather weakly absorbing for radiation at 21-cm wavelength.

The even lower mean particle densities observed for the lines of sight to some stars—about 0.01 cm$^{-3}$ or less—indicate that we cannot think of a uniform warm gas filling all the volume between the diffuse clouds. Instead, we must infer that this warm gas, like the cold gas in diffuse clouds, has a patchy distribution. There are extensive regions of the galactic disc in which the density is even less than it is within 15 light years of the Sun. As we shall see in chapters 6 and

7, these regions are probably occupied by hot gas, with a density much less than that of the warm gas. Thus the intercloud gas is of two types, one warm, one hot.

## THE DEUTERIUM-HYDROGEN RATIO

According to the Big Bang theory, summarized in chapter 1, helium and deuterium nuclei are formed a few minutes after creation, at a time when the temperature is falling below $10^{9°}$ K. The abundances of these nuclei relative to protons (hydrogen nuclei) depend on the particle density at that time. This dependence is particularly steep for deuterium, whose abundance falls dramatically as the density increases. At high densities, deuterons disappear by colliding with protons, neutrons, and other deuterons; these nuclear particles stick together and form additional helium nuclei. Thus if we know the primordial value of D/H, the deuterium-to-hydrogen ratio, we can determine the density of the Universe at this early stage.

This conclusion may be combined with another consequence of the Big Bang theory (see p. 9) concerning the ratio of photons to material particles. In any volume large enough to contain sufficient material for many galaxies, the ratio between the total number of photons present and the total number of protons plus neutrons remains constant after the first one-hundredth of a second. We know the present particle density of photons from direct microwave measures of the cosmic radiation field. The number of photons in each cubic centimeter at a temperature of $10^{9°}$ K is also known. Hence if we know the overall material density when deuterium and helium nuclei started to form (at a temperature of $10^{9°}$ K), we can compute immediately the present density of material in the Universe, smoothing stars and galaxies over the intervening space. In this way, a measurement of the primordial deuterium-hydrogen ratio gives indirectly the present density of the Universe.

A similar argument may be used for helium. However, the hydrogen-helium ratio depends much less sensitively on the density during element formation. This is because once helium nuclei are formed, nothing much happens to them through further nuclear collisions at the low densities characterizing this stage of the Big Bang. Hence a tenfold increase in density (when the temperature is $10^{9°}$ K) results in only a ten percent increase in the helium-hydrogen ratio, as compared with a twentyfold decrease in the deuterium-hydrogen ratio! It is the latter that depends sensitively on the present density of the Universe and provides the possibility of determining this density with some accuracy.

Determination of the average density of matter in the Universe would certainly be exciting. Is this density big enough for gravitational self-attraction to stop the expansion of the Universe? Or is the density so low that the galaxies will recede from each other forever? Can we indeed find the answer to these fundamental questions by measuring the ratio of deuterium to hydrogen?

There is one serious catch. How can we be certain that the D/H ratio in any place where we can measure it is the same as it was initially, some $10^{10}$ years ago? We know that neither the high D/H ratio observed on the Earth—about one in 6,000—nor the low value in the Sun—less than one in a million—are primordial. In the Sun deuterium is consumed by nuclear burning in the hot interior. The high terrestrial abundance of deuterium is thought to result from processes occurring when the Earth was formed by the gravitational self-attraction of many small, solid particles; deuterium, because of its greater mass, showed a greater tendency than hydrogen to adhere to these particles, thereby becoming a component of molecules containing heavier atoms. To what extent have other processes affected the relative abundance of deuterium and hydrogen is interstellar clouds? We cannot be certain.

We shall start out by assuming that the ratio of deuterium to hydrogen in the interstellar gas has retained its primordial value and discuss the Copernicus data and their interpretation. Then we shall return to the question of how this ratio may have changed in interstellar space during the hundred million centuries that have elapsed since creation.

To determine the deuterium-hydrogen ratio from Copernicus observations, absorption features may be used to find N(D) and N(H), the particle column densities of neutral deuterium and hydrogen respectively. The ratio of these two quantities equals n(D)/n(H), the ratio of the average particle densities per unit volume of these two types of atoms, which should be closely equal to the overall D/H ratio.

Although deuterium and ordinary hydrogen are similar chemically, their spectra are not quite identical. Thus the deuterium absorption features are shifted slightly—about 1/4 Å—to shorter wavelengths relative to the corresponding hydrogen features. The 1,216-Å feature—the strongest in the hydrogen spectrum, produced by an atomic transition up to the first excited orbit—is so wide that any deuterium absorption is usually completely masked. Transitions to more highly excited orbits produce weaker, narrower absorption features, at shorter wavelengths. The features produced by transitions to the next four excited orbits (at wavelengths ranging from

1,026 Å for the second excited orbit to 938 Å for the fifth) are narrow enough that hydrogen and deuterium absorption can be distinguished from each other and are often strong enough to permit accurate scans.

These features have been measured by *Copernicus* in the spectra of about a dozen stars. At these relatively short ultraviolet wavelengths, the reflectance of the two telescope mirrors and the spectrometer grating are relatively low, and only a very small fraction of the incoming photons gets counted. Hence observations at these wavelengths are limited to the brightest stars. Figure 4.5 shows a scan of the hydrogen and deuterium absorption features at 972 Å in the spectrum of Beta Centauri, the tenth brightest star in the sky, some 10° east of the Southern Cross. To obtain such data requires two of the distinctive characteristics of *Copernicus*—its sensitivity at

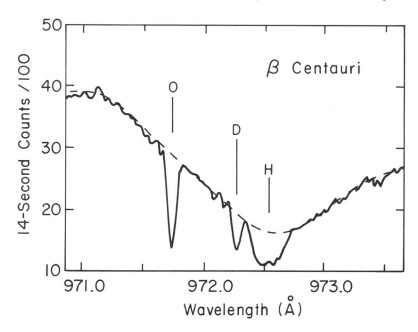

FIGURE 4.5 Scan of deuterium and hydrogen absorption features in Beta Centauri. For each absorption feature, a vertical line represents the central wavelength. The dashed line shows the source spectrum. The wide absorption feature is produced by hydrogen atoms in the stellar atmosphere. The narrow deuterium and hydrogen features are interstellar. These features are produced by electron transitions from the ground state up to the third excited orbit.

wavelengths less than 1,150 Å and its narrow measurement band. The broad hydrogen absorption feature in the source spectrum is clearly apparent.

To compute $N(D)$ from such a scan, the absorbed area, $W$, in the deuterium feature is measured, first dividing the photon count at each wavelength by the assumed count in the source spectrum (that is, the spectrum of the source in the absence of interstellar atomic absorption), as in figure 4.1. Then the curve of growth is used to determine whether the feature is approaching saturation, in which case $W$ gives only a lower limit on the deuterium column density. If the spread of atomic velocities along the line of sight were known, a theoretical curve could be used. Unfortunately this velocity information is not usually available beforehand. Instead, one must construct an empirical curve of growth from the observations.

To use the observations in this way, we take advantage of the fact that we have values of $W$ for several features produced by atoms that are all in the same ground state initially. If the absorbing power of an atom were the same for all transitions, the different absorption features would all have the same value of $W$. In fact, different transitions have different absorbing powers. Physicists have taken this into account by taking as a standard the absorbing power for an electron in an idealized atom, in which the electron absorbs and emits light at the maximum rate permitted by the laws of physics. For historical reasons, such an electron is sometimes referred to as a *classical electron oscillator*. The rate at which an actual atom absorbs radiation in one particular feature can be expressed as a fraction of the rate at which a classical electron oscillator would absorb. This fraction is called the *oscillator strength* and is generally denoted by the symbol $f$.

Each transition between two particular levels is characterized by its own value of $f$. For example, the value of $f$ for an upward transition of a hydrogen atom from its ground state to the first excited orbit the transition responsible for the 1,216 Å feature is 0.42. The same oscillator strength applies to the corresponding transition in deuterium. With increasing excitation of the upper state, $f$ decreases sharply, and for a transition from the ground state up to the fifth excited orbit in hydrogen (or deuterium), it is only 0.0078. Interestingly, the sum of the $f$ values for all the upward transitions from the ground state of hydrogen is exactly one, so in this sense the hydrogen atom is doing its best to resemble the idealized classical electron oscillator!

For some atoms, such as hydrogen, the values of $f$ can be computed from physical theory. For others, $f$ may be determined from laboratory measures. Once $f$ is known, the product $Nf$ for some absorption feature may be regarded as the *effective* column density—that is, the column density of classical electron oscillators required to produce the same absorption feature. If the absorbed area, $W_i$ is plotted against $Nf$ instead of $N$, different absorption features with identical $N$ but differing $f$ may be combined in a single curve of growth (provided they have nearly the same wavelength).

Use of this technique to determine $N(D)$ (to which we shall sometimes refer in the next few paragraphs simply as $N$) is illustrated by figure 4.6, in which a curve of growth is plotted for the four deuterium features observed in Alpha Crucis, the brightest, most southerly, star in the Southern Cross. The theoretical, solid curve provides an excellent fit to the data. This theoretical curve of growth corresponds

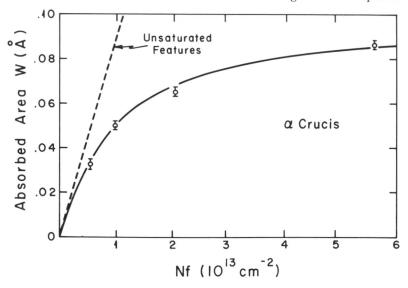

FIGURE 4.6 Curve of growth for deuterium in Alpha Crucis. The circles give observed values of $W$ for four interstellar deuterium absorption features. The vertical bars above and below each circle indicate estimated (rms) observational errors. The horizontal scale equals the product of $f$, the known oscillator strength for each feature, and $N(D)$, the column density of neutral deuterium in the line of sight to Alpha Crucis. To obtain the best agreement with the theoretical curve (computed for a velocity spread of 5 km sec$^{-1}$), $N(D)$ was set equal to $7 \times 10^{14}$ cm$^{-2}$. The dashed line shows $W$ for unsaturated absorption features.

to a wavelength of 1,000 Å and a thermal distribution of velocities at a gas temperature of 6,000° K. At this temperature the value of V, the average (rms) spread of random velocities in the line of sight, is about 5 km sec⁻¹. In plotting the observed values of W, the column density N(D) is taken to be $7 \times 10^{14}$ cm⁻². Thus the good agreement between the theoretical curve and the plotted points provides a determination of V and N(D). (A more exact calculation, taking into account the different wavelengths of these four absorption features, alters V and N slightly.)

The detailed techniques for actually finding the best-fitting theoretical curve need not concern us here. However, a closer examination of figure 4.6 may help to clarify the physical principles that underlie the determination of N(D). The dashed line in the figure shows the general relationship between W and Nf (computed for a wavelength of 1,000 Å) for unsaturated features—that is, those for which different atoms do not get in each other's way, so that each is absorbing photons from the full source spectrum, which is not appreciably weakened. As we have seen, a feature is unsaturated if the depth of the feature (equal to one minus the relative intensity, r) is sufficiently small.

It is evident that saturation is most serious for the strongest feature plotted—that produced by the deuterium transition from the ground state up to the second excited orbit. The rather small effect of saturation on the two weakest features is evident from the fact that W varies almost proportionally with f for these two lowest points. A proportional variation requires that a straight line through these points would also pass through the point where the two axes intersect, where $W = Nf = 0$. Examination of the figure shows that this condition is nearly satisfied. (This result would be unchanged by adopting a different value for N, which can be handled by simply multiplying all the numbers on the horizontal scale by a constant factor.) We conclude that for the weakest feature, the effect of saturation is rather small. If N is determined from this feature (using the relationship shown by the dashed line), the column density is found to be $5 \times 10^{14}$ cm⁻² instead of the somewhat higher value of $7 \times 10^{14}$ cm⁻² obtained with the use of the solid, theoretical curve, which takes saturation into account. For the strongest feature, in contrast, neglect of saturation gives a value of N(D) that is incorrect by a spectacular amount.

We see that the empirical curve of growth plotted in figure 4.6 is based on absorption features all of which have the same value of N but different values of f. One of the chief advantages of such an empirical curve is that it indicates when saturation is weak, and thus when reliable values of $N$ can be obtained. When saturation is strong for all the measured features, only a lower limit for $N$ can normally be trusted. This topic has been discussed here in detail because such curves are used in much of the *Copernicus* research described in the next two chapters.

For hydrogen atoms, the curve of growth is not needed to find the column densities. As noted above, $N(H)$ is best determined from the profiles of the wings, which are usually evident for transitions to the first few excited states. The curve of growth for hydrogen is still of some use, however, in that it gives information about the average spread of velocities in the line of sight, and thus of the gas temperature. Along the lines of sight to some stars, the temperature determined in this way is roughly equal to the 6,000° K found for deuterium, indicating that in these regions the absorption features are in fact broadened by random thermal motions, rather than by large-scale eddies and other turbulent motions in the gas.

The general value of D/H found from these studies is $1.5 \times 10^{-5}$, or one deuterium atom for every 70,000 hydrogen atoms. If this ratio is assumed to be primordial, the present smoothed density of the Universe is about $5 \times 10^{-31}$ gm cm$^{-3}$, about a tenth of the value required to stop the expansion of the Universe by self-gravitational attraction. Some hydrogen has been processed through stars, condensing in protostellar clouds and subsequently being ejected again in one form or another. Since nuclear burning is much more rapid for deuterium than hydrogen, any deuterium passing through a star would doubtless be destroyed. Hence the primordial D/H ratio may have exceeded its present value—perhaps by as much as twice. In this case, the present density of the Universe might be even lower—about $3 \times 10^{-31}$ gm cm$^{-3}$.

On the other hand it is also possible that almost all of the observed deuterium was created more recently, perhaps in supernova explosions or other cataclysms. This suggestion runs into the difficulty that all production mechanisms suggested so far produce certain other elements (notably lithium, beryllium, and boron), to an extent that is in disagreement with the observations. Perhaps the theorists have not yet thought hard enough about this problem!

Variations in D/H between different lines of sight might give some clue as to whether deuterium is being destroyed or created within the Galaxy. Such variations have in fact been found but are not much bigger than the errors of the determinations. Toward a few stars D/H is about half its average value. This might be understood as gas that has recently been shot out from stars, as a result of which its deuterium is depleted. In two stars, including Alpha Crucis (see figure 4.6) D/H is nearly twice the average. An even larger value of D/H in some smaller regions might provide more definite confirmation of recent deuterium formation. At the moment all these results on D/H appear suggestive rather than conclusive.

Not infrequently in science, just when we seem to be on the verge of simple, sweeping conclusions, more refined observations indicate that Nature is more complicated than we had supposed. Fortunately, broad progress in our general understanding does continue, but often at the cost of increasing complication in the details.

## SUMMARY

The ratio of gas to dust is reasonably constant in most clouds, with observed variations generally less than a factor of two.

The mean particle density of hydrogen within 300 light years of the Sun is about 0.1 atom $cm^{-3}$, about a tenth of the average value found in the galactic disc within a larger volume extending out to 3,000 light years. In some regions this particle density of neutral hydrogen atoms is even smaller, at most 0.01 $cm^{-3}$. These variations confirm the very patchy distribution of the interstellar gas.

The average ratio of deuterium to hydrogen atoms in the interstellar gas is about $1.5 \times 10^{-5}$. If this abundance is primordial, resulting from nuclear reactions during the Big Bang, the present density of the Universe is about one-tenth of the value required to close the Universe and ultimately stop its expansion. Small variations in this ratio observed between different regions suggest that recent processes may have altered the primordial abundance ratio.

# 5

# Clouds of Molecular Hydrogen

Hydrogen atoms can stick together in pairs to form hydrogen molecules. Such $H_2$ molecules are each composed of two protons around which two electrons are rapidly moving. The hydrogen atom is the simplest atom known, and the simplest molecule is that composed of two such atoms.

Molecular hydrogen is important in interstellar research for two reasons. First, hydrogen constitutes most of the gas between the stars, and whether its atoms remain single or combine in pairs affects the interstellar gas in many respects—temperature, chemical evolution, and in particular its condensation into new stars. Second, hydrogen molecules produce many absorption features, and comparison of these different features gives detailed information on the physical state of the interstellar gas. Studies of these interstellar $H_2$ features constitute one of the most exciting uses of the *Copernicus* satellite.

Before discussing these observations and their interpretation, we first look at certain general characteristics of the spectrum produced by $H_2$ molecules—in particular the variety of features appearing in the $H_2$ spectrum and the information that can be extracted from them. A molecule, like an atom, will absorb or emit photons at certain wavelengths, each corresponding to a transition between two particular molecular states. In a hydrogen atom there is only the electron to consider, and transitions between two particular electronic states will produce only one feature in the spectrum. In a hydrogen molecule, however, the motions of the two protons become important. These two relatively heavy particles can circle around each other, producing a rotation of the molecule as a whole. Also, they can vibrate back and forth along the line between them, producing a pulsation in the length of the molecule. The overall state of the molecule depends not only on the electronic state, but also on the state of motion of the two protons—that is, on the rotational and vibrational states. When the electronic state of a molecule changes, the vibrational and rotational states usually change at the same time, with a single photon being emitted or absorbed. (If the molecule is in the ground electronic state, a photon can be emitted in a vibrational-rotational transition.) Transitions between two particular vibrational states, accompanied by a simultaneous transition between two electronic states, produce a group of features called a *band*. Within a single band each feature corresponds to a transition between two rotational states. In a typical stellar spectrum viewed by *Copernicus*, about a dozen separate bands produced by interstellar $H_2$ can be measured, each band containing five to ten different absorption features.

For interstellar studies, an important characteristic of the $H_2$ spectrum is that in each $H_2$ band only one absorption feature is produced by a molecule in its ground rotational state, that in which the molecule does not rotate. In all the other features, the photons are absorbed by molecules in excited rotational states. As we have seen in chapter 3, most atoms cascade down to the ground state very rapidly and are generally in this state when they absorb light. The same thing happens in molecules for electronic and vibrational states, and molecular absorption almost always occurs from states with no electronic or vibrational excitation. For $H_2$ rotational states, however, the situation is quite different.

Spontaneous downward transitions from excited $H_2$ rotational states with no electronic or vibrational excitation occur very slowly. Downward transitions from the first such excited state, with spontaneous emission of a photon, are so rare that they may be ignored entirely. Molecules in this state will remain there until excited by a passing photon or perturbed by a collision with a passing atom. From the second excited rotational state, the hydrogen molecule can jump spontaneously to the ground state, emitting a photon (in the infrared), but the time required averages about a thousand years. With increasing rotational excitation the spontaneous downward transition time becomes shorter; for the sixth excited rotational state, this transition time amounts to about a year, longer than for most of the states with vibrational or electronic excitation. As a result of these long lifetimes, as they are called, an appreciable fraction of interstellar $H_2$ molecules are in these rotational states at any one time. It is the measurement of this rotationally excited fraction that serves as a primary source of information on the physical conditions in the gas, such as particle density and temperature, that are responsible for the rotational excitation.

The first section of this chapter gives a more detailed description of the interstellar $H_2$ spectrum. This section may be helpful to readers who have some interest or background in these topics but is not vital for a general understanding of the remaining material. A subsequent section describes how the *Copernicus* data determine what fraction of the hydrogen is molecular in an interstellar cloud and also accounts theoretically for the observed values of this fraction.

The third section shows how $H_2$ observations with *Copernicus* have given values for the temperature and density of the gas, as well as the intensity of the ultraviolet starlight striking the cloud. At the end of the chapter we look at some of the many ways in which $H_2$ molecules affect the chemical equilibrium and development of interstellar clouds.

## THE INTERSTELLAR $H_2$ SPECTRUM

Although all molecular spectra are complicated by the fact that three different states (electronic, vibrational, and rotational) can change during a typical transition, the $H_2$ interstellar absorption spectrum is simplified by several circumstances. As we have seen, so very few molecules are in excited states of electronic motion or heavy ion vibration that absorption by such molecules can be ignored. A further simplification specific for $H_2$ is that only one excited electronic state need be considered; all $H_2$ absorption features that have been studied systematically by *Copernicus* arise as a result of one particular electronic transition, that from the ground state up to the first excited electronic state of the bound molecule. Hence the ultraviolet $H_2$ spectrum consists of a single series of bands, each band corresponding to a transition from the ground vibrational state to one of several excited vibrational states. We denote by the integer $v$ (the vibrational *quantum number*) the degree of excitation of the vibrational state; thus $v$ is 0 for the ground vibrational state and is 1, 2, 3, . . . for the first, second, third, . . excited vibrational states. For a transition between two states, subscripts $l$ and $u$ will be used to denote values for the lower and upper states, respectively. Under interstellar conditions, $v_l$ is 0 for almost all molecules, and each absorption band corresponds to vibrational transitions in which $v$ increases from 0 to some particular value, $v_u$.

Within each band, absorption by $H_2$ molecules in different excited rotational states produces a variety of separate absorption features. We denote by the integer $J$ (the rotational quantum number) the degree of excitation of the rotational state; $J$ is 0 for the ground rotational state with no rotation and is 1, 2, 3 . . . . for the first, second, third. . . . excited rotational states. Here we use $J$ to denote the degree of rotational excitation for the lower state of a transition, omitting the subscript $l$. If the upper state is excited by the absorption of a photon, the degree of rotational excitation of the lower state is $J \pm 1$; that is, $J$ can normally increase or decrease by at most one unit during a transition produced by absorption of a single photon.

The character of the $H_2$ spectrum depends on the energies involved in these three types of transitions—electronic, vibrational, and rotational. As we have seen earlier, the photon energy, $E$ (equal, by Planck's law, to $hc/\lambda$, or, in electron Volts, to $12,400/\lambda$, where $\lambda$ is in Ångstroms), is the difference in energy between the upper and lower states. For a molecular transition this difference is the sum of three different energies, each of which is an energy difference between the initial and final states. First, there is the change in the electronic energy, generally the dominant contribution in ultraviolet molecular spectra; for the one $H_2$ electronic transition that we consider here, this excitation energy is about 11.2 eV. Second, there is the change in the vibrational energy of the positive atomic nuclei, whose excitation energy—the difference in energy between the excited and ground state—is roughly proportional to $v$, ranging in $H_2$ from 0.16 eV for $v_u = 1$ up to 1.4 eV for $v_u = 10$. Third, there is the change in the rotational energy; for $H_2$ the rotational excitation energy in the lower electronic state amounts to 0.015 eV for $J = 1$, increasing roughly as $J^2$.

In order to apply these results to interstellar $H_2$ absorption features, we look now at some Copernicus data. Figure 5.1 shows the spectrum of the bright, hot star Zeta Ophiuchi over a wavelength interval of 8 Å, which includes the principal $H_2$ absorption features in the $v_u = 4$ band. It took about an hour and a half of scanning with Copernicus to obtain data plotted here. Since only about a third of the time can normally be used for observing (because of stellar occultation by the Earth and other practical problems), about four hours was needed to obtain these observations. The vertical lines in the figure show the centers of the various absorption features. One feature from the adjacent $v_u = 5$ band evidently appears in the $v_u = 4$ band. Only one of the eight observed $H_2$ features in this figure is from the ground rotational state ($J = 0$); absorption is produced by molecules excited as high as the fifth rotational state ($J = 5$). For molecules

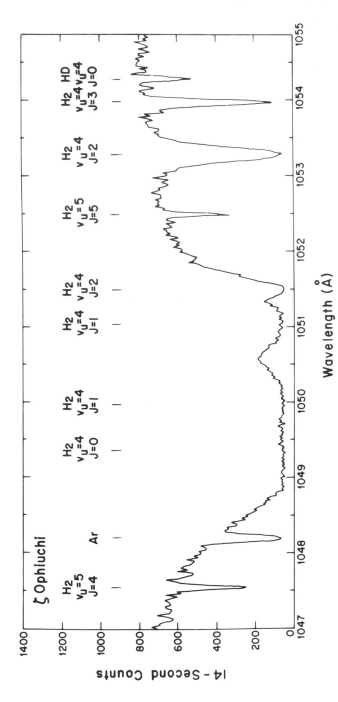

FIGURE 5.1. Interstellar $H_2$ absorption features in Zeta Ophiuchi. All the absorption features in this *Copernicus* spectrum are produced by interstellar $H_2$ (or HD) molecules except for the one feature produced by neutral argon (Ar) atoms. The different wavelengths of these $H_2$ features result from different rotational and vibrational energies of the lower and upper states involved in each transition; the numbers $J$ and $v_u$ denote the different rotational and vibrational states, respectively, of the absorbing molecules.

that are intially in the $J^{th}$ excited rotational state, a pair of absorption features within each band is produced, corresponding to $J$ increasing or decreasing by one unit in the upward transition. Only a single absorption feature appears if $J = 0$ in the lower state.

The values given above for the different excitation energies in $H_2$ provide a straightforward explanation of the wavelengths shown for the different features in this figure. For the feature with $J = 0$, the energy of the photon absorbed is 11.2 eV as a result of the electronic transition, plus about 0.6 eV vibrational excitation energy for $v_u = 4$. This total energy difference of 11.8 eV corresponds to the wavelength of 1,050 Å shown in the figure. The small energy change associated with rotational excitation produces the separation of about 1 Å between the different absorption features within each band, with somewhat greater separation for greater $J$. The separation between different bands results from the difference in vibrational energy; an additional energy of 0.15 eV at 1,050 Å decreases the wavelength by about 13 Å. Evidently the wavelength separation between bands somewhat exceeds the separation between individual features within a band.

The interstellar $H_2$ spectrum, as illustrated in figure 5.1, shows many strong features, a number of which appear in the spectra of most of the stars observed with *Copernicus*. When this equipment was being designed and built, during the 1960s, there was no evidence whatever for the presence of $H_2$ in interstellar space, although extensive theoretical discussions, extending back to Sir Arthur Eddington in 1937, had suggested that this molecule should be abundant. Early in 1970, almost a year and a half before *Copernicus* was launched, interstellar $H_2$ was detected for the first time by G. R. Carruthers, using a sounding rocket which, during its few minutes above the atmosphere, recorded the spectrum of one star, employing a measurement band with a width of about 2 Å, small enough to show the major $H_2$ absorption features. At the time of the *Copernicus* launch, it was reassuring to us to know that there were interesting and important measurements on $H_2$ to be made with our more precise equipment, if only it would operate as planned!

One conspicuous aspect of figure 5.1 is the great strength of the features due to absorption by $H_2$ molecules in the $J = 0$ and $J = 1$ rotational states, which are very much more populated than the higher rotational states. The wings of these features are prominent, especially the unblended wing at the shorter wavelength, produced mostly by the $J = 0$ feature. As we shall see in the following section, these wings may be used for determining column densities.

## FRACTION OF HYDROGEN
## IN MOLECULAR FORM

The *Copernicus* telescope-spectrometer has been used to determine $N(H_2)$, the column density of molecular hydrogen, along the lines of sight to about eighty stars. Here we see how these observations indicate that the fraction of hydrogen in molecular form is almost vanishingly small for transparent clouds but rises to nearly 1 for more opaque clouds. We shall also see how this dramatic result can be understood theoretically.

For about sixty of the stars measured, the $H_2$ column densities along the lines of sight exceeded $10^{18}$ cm$^{-2}$. Most of the hydrogen molecules are in the ground rotational state ($J = 0$) or the first excited rotational state ($J = 1$) when they absorb an ultraviolet photon. In this chapter we shall denote by $N(0)$ and $N(1)$ the column densities for $H_2$ molecules in these two rotational states; except for an exceedingly tiny fraction, all these molecules are in the ground electronic and vibrational states. Evidently $N(H_2)$ is the sum of $N(0)$ and $N(1)$, plus some small contribution from more highly excited rotational states such as $N(2)$ and $N(3)$.

For $N(0)$ and $N(1)$ each equal to about $10^{18}$ cm$^{-2}$ or more, absorption features produced by molecules in these two rotational states generally show strong wings. By fitting with a theoretical curve the detailed profiles of the features in any one of the different bands (with different values of $v_u$), values of $N(0)$ and $N(1)$ can be obtained, just as $N(H)$ was found by fitting the detailed profile of the 1,216-Å absorption feature to a theoretical curve. As shown in figure 5.1, each band includes three such strong absorption features, which overlap somewhat, but in principle this overlap introduces no real problem.

For the remaining stars observed, the column densities $N(0)$ and $N(1)$ were less than $10^{18}$ cm$^{-2}$. For most of these spectra, detailed curves of growth were used to determine the column densities. As shown in the next section, these determinations, based on many different absorption features in each star, yielded values of $N(J)$ for higher $J$, as well as for $J = 0$ and $J = 1$. Finally, for five of the stars, the equivalent widths were so small that the features could safely be assumed to be on the proportional section of the curve of growth, and values of $Nf$ could be determined immediately from the values of $W$, the absorbed area, observed for each feature.

Values of $N(H)$ are available for all but a very few of these stars, obtained from the profile of the 1,216-Å feature. As in chapter 4, we may add $N(H)$ to $2N(H_2)$ to give $N(H_{Tot})$, the overall total number of neutral hydrogen atoms in the line of sight, including those in $H_2$ molecules as well as the separate atoms. Figure 5.2 is a plot of $N(H_2)$ against $N(H_{Tot})$. Because of the enormous range covered by $N(H_2)$, this quantity is plotted on a geometric (or logarithmic) scale, with values on the vertical scale increasing by successive powers of 10, as in a geometric progression. The dashed line shows what the values of $N(H_2)$ would be if all hydrogen were molecular that is, if $N(H_{Tot}) = 2N(H_2)$.

This figure indicates that for relatively low values of $N(H_{Tot})$—less than about $10^{20}$ cm$^{-2}$—the fraction of hydrogen in molecular form is very small—less than one part in about $10^5$. For large $N(H_{Tot})$—about $10^{21}$ cm$^{-2}$—at least ten percent of the hydrogen is usually in molecules, and generally more. For intermediate $N(H_{Tot})$, the fraction of hydrogen in molecular form may cover a wide range of values, with a tendency to be either small (less than a thousandth) or greater than a tenth. This state of affairs has been described in an exaggerated, but striking, way as "all or nothing"; that is, either all of the

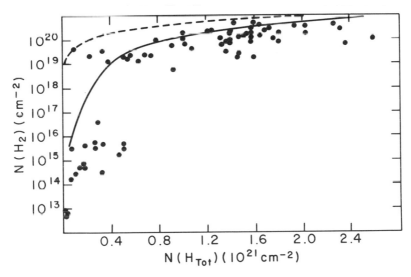

FIGURE 5.2 Observed $H_2$ column densities. The dots represent individual values of the $H_2$ column density in the line of sight, $N(H_2)$, plotted against the observed overall hydrogen column densities (including $H_2$). The dashed line shows what the values would be if all the hydrogen were molecular. The solid line shows what the values would be for clouds of differing thickness but with an internal density, $n(H_{Tot})$, of 60 cm$^{-3}$.

hydrogen is molecular, or none of it is. A more correct description would be "much or little."

Let us turn now to a consideration of how this remarkable result is to be understood in terms of scientific laws. Theorists have shown that the explanation is straightforward once we understand the processes by which $H_2$ molecules are first formed from individual atoms and then dissociated back into separate atoms. It is the competition between these two processes, formation and dissociation, that determines how much hydrogen will be in the molecular state.

The combination of two hydrogen atoms to form a molecule is believed to occur on the surfaces of dust grains. This point of view is consistent with the behavior of hydrogen gas in the laboratory. A gas of hydrogen atoms will remain in atomic form unless a catalyst is present. Glass is not a good catalyst for $H_2$ formation, but metals can be. What happens is that hydrogen atoms stick to the surface of such a catalyst, migrating slowly from one place to the next. In the course of these migrations, two hydrogen atoms can encounter each other, in which case the presence of the catalyst makes it possible for the two atoms to become paired. The molecule that is formed can then escape from the catalyst and move freely through the gas. This bonding together of two atoms does not occur when the atoms meet by themselves but requires the close presence of a third body, the catalyst.

The total surface area of dust grains that is available for this catalytic action is known from the measured absorption of starlight (especially at shorter wavelengths) caused by these solid particles. Theorists compute that for a plausible cloud density of 20 hydrogen atoms $cm^{-3}$ half the hydrogen atoms will have combined to form $H_2$ molecules in about thirty million years. This is a long time, even for an interstellar cloud; quite a bit can happen to a cloud during this period. Nevertheless, the tendency toward formation of $H_2$ molecules is a steady one, and almost all interstellar hydrogen would be in the form of molecules by now if there were no disruptive process at work dissociating them.

In fact there is one important process that dissociates hydrogen molecules very effectively. This disruptive mechanism is the result of absorption of ultraviolet photons in the many $H_2$ absorption features studied with *Copernicus*. Absorption of a photon leaves the $H_2$ molecule in an excited electronic state. The excitation energy of this state, as pointed out above, is, about 11 eV, much more than the 4.5 eV required to pull the two atoms apart. If this energy is transferred to the two protons, they will separate immediately, each taking one electron along, forming two separate neutral hydrogen atoms.

As it happens, it is possible for enough of this electron energy to be transferred to the protons that the molecule promptly dissociates. This will happen if the downward electronic transition back to the ground electronic state leaves the molecule in a highly excited vibrational state, in which the energy of vibration of the two protons is sufficient to tear them apart. (This will happen if $v_1$, the vibrational quantum number of the lower state, exceeds 14 ) Calculations show that for every nine $H_2$ molecules that absorb ultraviolet photons, one molecule will dissociate in this way.

How fast is this dissociation? We know the intensity of ultraviolet radiation from the stars, and we can compute how often a hydrogen molecule will absorb a photon and be left in an excited electronic state. For conditions near the Sun, it turns out that a single hydrogen molecule will be excited in this way once every 60 years. If one out of every nine such absorptions produces dissociation, the average time to dissociate will be about 500 years. Evidently if hydrogen atoms each spend $3 \times 10^7$ years in the single state on the average and only 500 years in molecular form, the ratio of the times spent in atomic and molecular form is $(3 \times 10^7)/(5 \times 10^2)$ or $6 \times 10^4$.

The ratio of hydrogen atoms in the single state to those bound in molecules will equal this ratio of times spent in the two states. The principle involved is illustrated by a simple example; if the average person spends as much time exhaling as inhaling, then at any one time on the Earth as a whole, the number of people exhaling will just equal the number inhaling. Since a hydrogen atom spends 60,000 times as long as a free particle as it does bound in a hydrogen molecule, the ratio of free hydrogen atoms to those in molecules is 60,000 to 1. Since it takes two atoms to make a $H_2$ molecule, the ratio of $n(H)$ to $n(H_2)$ is $1.2 \times 10^5$, giving about $10^{-5}$ for the ratio of $H_2$ to $H$ (that is, for the ratio of $n(H_2)$ to $n(H)$).

This theoretical ratio of $H_2$ to $H$ depends on the gas density, since the time a neutral hydrogen atom must wait before it forms a hydrogen molecule is inversely proportional to the density. On the other hand, the time a hydrogen molecule must wait before it dissociates is independent of density, provided the number of ultraviolet photons present stays the same. Hence if a cloud is considered to have a particle density as low as 2 atom $cm^{-3}$, one tenth of the value assumed above, then the ratio of $H_2$ molecules to unbound atoms falls to $10^{-6}$. This is about the lowest value of the ratio shown in figure 5.2.

This analysis explains the lowest points in figure 5.2, provided they are associated with rather inconspicuous clouds in which both the particle density $n(H)$ and the column density $N(H)$ are unusually low. To explain the upper points, we must take into account the absorption that $H_2$ molecules produce in the ultraviolet radiation striking the cloud. In the outer regions of a cloud, into which the ultraviolet radiation penetrates without much absorption, the ratio of bound to free hydrogen atoms is indeed small. However, the resultant total $H_2$ column density from the surface down into the central regions of the cloud can be large enough to absorb much of the ultraviolet radiation reaching the cloud in the wavelength regions of the $H_2$ absorption features. As a result, $H_2$ molecules in the central regions of the cloud will be shielded by the molecules in the surrounding regions and can avoid dissociation back into separate atoms for millions of years.

Let us put some numbers into this argument. We have seen that the hydrogen column density through a typical diffuse cloud is about $4 \times 10^{20}$ cm$^{-2}$. For a cloud density of 20 atoms cm$^{-3}$, the ratio of bound to free hydrogen atoms computed above (neglecting any shielding against ultraviolet starlight) was roughly $2 \times 10^{-5}$, giving $4 \times 10^{15}$ molecules cm$^{-2}$ for $N(H_2)$ along a line of sight through the cloud. This is a sufficient number of molecules to cause strong absorption in the prominent $H_2$ features, reducing the ultraviolet intensity at the center of these features dramatically and increasing thereby both the lifetime of an $H_2$ molecule before dissociation and the relative number of these molecules. As a result $N(H_2)$ will be significantly increased above $4 \times 10^{15}$ molecules cm$^{-2}$.

Quantitative theories of these effects have been worked out, following the lines of reasoning outlined in the last few paragraphs, and the resultant values of $N(H_2)$ have been computed for particular overall values of the column density, $N(H_{Tot})$, all the way through the cloud. As $N(H_{Tot})$ increases, the opacity in the strong $H_2$ features becomes larger and larger; dissociation can now be produced by the photons in the weaker features, whose absorbing power (measured by $Nf$) is relatively small, or by photons whose wavelengths are far out in the wings of the stronger features, to which the molecule is relatively insensitive. A number of complicating additional factors, including absorption by dust grains, have also been included in the theory. The solid line in figure 5.2 shows a resultant theoretical curve, computed for an overall hydrogen particle density of 60 cm$^{-3}$ and a particular assumed field of interstellar ultraviolet radiation.

Close agreement is certainly not to be expected between the observations and the theoretical curve drawn for one set of conditions. The gas densities within clouds vary tremendously, and the rate at which ultraviolet photons reach a cloud should depend very sensitively on where the cloud happens to be located with respect to bright, hot stars. These variations should produce the largest effects on $N(H_2)$ when $N(H_{Tot})$ is relatively small and the theoretical curve has a very steep slope. This expectation is confirmed by the scatter of the observed points, whose vertical distance from the solid theoretical curve is greatest at the left-hand side of the figure.

Since the theory seems to explain the trend of the data in a physically reasonable way, and since there seems to be no plausible alternative, this account of $H_2$ formation and destruction has been widely accepted as correct. Probably it is. However, since there is no precise numerical agreement with observation, the theory is not conclusively established.

## PHYSICAL CONDITIONS WITHIN THE CLOUDS

In some ways the hydrogen molecule seems made to order as a probe of the interstellar gas. The molecule has a variety of rotational states (with no vibrational or electronic excitation) that have low excitation energies and persist for many years before the molecule emits radiation spontaneously and performs a transition to the ground rotational state (or to the $J = 1$ state). Under interstellar conditions, an appreciable number of $H_2$ molecules are excited to these high-$J$ states as a result of two processes—collisions with atoms and other molecules and spontaneous downward transitions into these states following absorption of an ultraviolet photon. Measurement of the relative numbers of molecules in each of these rotational states gives information on these two processes, and thus on the particle density of the colliding particles, on the random velocities or temperatures of these particles, and on the intensity of ultraviolet radiation—that is, on the rate at which ultraviolet photons reach the molecule and are absorbed.

If there were only one absorption feature produced by molecules in each rotational state, it would be difficult to determine for each $J$ the value of $N(J)$, the column density for $H_2$ molecules excited to the $J^{th}$ rotational state. As we have already seen, unless an absorption feature has wings, possible saturation makes the relevant column density uncertain if only a single feature is measured with imperfect resolution and accuracy. Fortunately, there are many features that are due to absorption by molecules in each rotational state; every band contains one or two such features, and as many as a dozen different $H_2$ bands can be measured with Copernicus.

This multiplicity of features produced by molecules in each rotational state is useful to us, because the transitions that cause different features have different absorbing powers. We have seen in the preceding chapter that the absorbing power of a transition is measured by an oscillator strength, $f$. It is fortunate for us that different bands give features with different $f$ values. For example, for the feature produced by absorption from the ground rotational state ($J = 0$), the oscillator strength equals $1.7 \times 10^{-3}$ for the $v_u = 0$ band (corresponding to a transition in which no vibrational excitation occurs). For the $v_u = 1$, $J = 0$ feature, $f$ increases to $6.0 \times 10^{-3}$, and for $v_u$ between 3 and 11 (again with $J = 0$), it increases to about $2 \times 10^{-2}$. In each band, similar $f$ values apply for each pair of transitions from states of higher initial rotational energy (higher $J$). Thanks to this tenfold range of $f$ values, a separate curve of growth can be constructed for each initial rotational state. In this way the effects of saturation can be detected and corrected for, and the column density $N(J)$ can be found for $H_2$ molecules in each rotational state.

This use of $H_2$ molecules to probe conditions has had a number of applications. The one we shall describe first is the determination of the gas temperature. This determination is based on the ratio of $N(1)$ to $N(0)$, the column densities of $H_2$ molecules in the first excited rotational state and the ground state (with no vibrational or electronic excitation), respectively. For this particular application we need not concern ourselves with saturation and curves of growth, since for the situations of interest the spectrum features due to absorption from these two rotational states show prominent wings, as in figure 5.1. Hence $N(1)$ and $N(0)$ can be determined rather accurately by fitting the observed profiles, as discussed above.

How can the gas temperature be determined from the ratio of $N(1)$ to $N(0)$? We have already seen that there are no direct radiative transitions between the states $J = 0$ and $J = 1$. The relative numbers of molecules in these two states are determined by two other mechanisms. First, there are collisions with passing atoms and other molecules, which can either excite hydrogen molecules to higher rotational states or de-excite them to lower states. Second, photon absorption may dissociate the molecule which, under steady-state conditions, will be replaced by another molecule, newly formed on a dust grain; the $J$ value of the new molecule may differ from that of the old. If $N(H_2)$ exceeds about $10^{18}$ cm$^{-2}$, which is also a condition for the $J = 0$ and $J = 1$ absorption features to show strong wings, absorption will have reduced so strongly the number of passing ultraviolet photons which can excite $H_2$ molecules that this second mechanism becomes relatively unimportant. In this situation, $N(1)/N(0)$ is determined entirely by collisions, which produce transitions back and forth between these two rotational states. (It is actually only certain collisions, those with protons, that produce these transitions, but this point is not essential to our present discussion.)

In this situation, with collisions the dominant process for both excitation and de-excitation, the ratio $N(1)/N(0)$ depends only on the temperature, which can therefore be determined from a measurement of this ratio. The basic physical reason for the temperature dependence is that excitation can be produced only if the kinetic energy of random thermal motion in the colliding particles exceeds the excitation energy of 0.015 eV—the difference in energy between the $J = 0$ and $J = 1$ states. Although different molecules in a gas at some temperature will have widely different random velocities and corresponding kinetic energies, only a small fraction of the molecules will have kinetic energies much greater than the average. The average kinetic energy, which is proportional to the temperature, equals 0.015 eV when the temperature is 115° K. Hence, if $T$ is much less than 115° K, the average kinetic energy is much less than 0.015 eV; the fraction of collisions that have an energy of motion greater than 0.015 eV is then very small, and the probability of excitation from the $J = 0$ to the $J = 1$ state is correspondingly small.

By contrast, de-excitation from $J = 1$ back to $J = 0$ does not depend very strongly on the energy of motion of the colliding particles, and its probability remains high even at low temperatures. Hence, if the average temperature of the gas falls much below 110° K, $H_2$ molecules will tend to accumulate in the $J = 0$ state, with a resultant low value for the ratio $N(1)/N(0)$. On the other hand, when the temperature of the gas rises above 110° K, most collisions can produce either excitation or de-excitation, and $N(1)$ will have a value comparable to $N(0)$. Thus the measured ratio $N(1)/N(0)$ provides a useful thermometer for the gas in an interstellar cloud. (Quantitatively, $N(1)/N(0) = Ke^{-170/T}$, where $e$ is again the base of the Napierian logarithms, and $K$ is a constant for the $H_2$ molecule.) As shown in the previous paragraph, the chief proviso for the use of this thermometer is that $N(H_2)$ be large enough to produce high opacity in the ultraviolet absorption features, so that there is no appreciable excitation of $H_2$ molecules by photons.

This thermometer has been used to determine gas temperatures in clouds along the lines of sight to sixty-one stars. Individual values range from 45 to 128° K, with an average of about 80° K, or − 315° F. This is about the same result as that obtained from the 21-cm observations and greatly increases our confidence that the interpretation of both sets of data is essentially correct. There are often many pitfalls in the path of scientific research—unknown systematic errors in the observations, unsuspected physical phenomena at work—and it is vastly reassuring to obtain good numerical agreement between results obtained in entirely different ways.

There is another powerful method for using $H_2$ measures as a probe of the interstellar gas, giving values for both the hydrogen density and the intensity of ultraviolet radiation. This method uses the values of $N(J)$—the column density of molecules in the $J$th excited rotational state—for higher $J$, in addition to the values of $N(0)$ and $N(1)$ used above. As before, essentially all the molecules included in $N(J)$ will be in the ground electronic and vibrational states. Let us consider what physical processes determine the *population ratios*—the ratios between the column densities for different values of $J$. Once we understand what is going on, it is then straightforward to interpret the observed population ratios in terms of certain gas properties.

In this more general case, absorption of ultraviolet photons provides one of two important mechanisms for exciting molecules to the upper rotational states. The process of ultraviolet absorption, followed by downward cascading from state to state, starting with an excited electronic state, can take a molecule that was in a low-$J$ state before photon absorption and put it in a high-$J$ state when it arrives back down at the ground vibrational and electronic states. The second mechanism for exciting molecules to high-$J$ states is provided by collisions, which, as we have already seen, can produce direct transitions between states of different $J$. De-excitation of these rotational states down to states of lower $J$ can also be produced by either of these mechanisms, as well as by the emission of infrared photons, with accompanying spontaneous downward transitions. It is important to note that these particular spontaneous radiative transitions (in which $J$ must always decrease by 2, as it turns out) occur at a constant rate for a rotationally excited molecule in a particular $J$ state, a rate that is independent of physical conditions in the surrounding medium.

Let us now consider what happens to the various population ratios as physical conditions change. As one limiting case, let both the ultraviolet radiation intensity and the particle density fall to very low values. The two sources of excitation for $H_2$ rotational levels, absorption of ultraviolet photons and collisions with atoms or other molecules, are now very weak. Any $H_2$ molecule placed in the second excited rotational state or higher will in due course emit a photon and make a transition to a lower rotational state. Hence the population ratios $N(2)/N(0)$ and $N(3)/N(1)$ will fall to low values. Conversely, we know that if these ratios are low, the two processes that produce excitation must be weak.

What happens when both these processes are active is a more subtle question. To answer this, detailed computations of these population ratios have been made under different assumptions for the three parameters: gas temperature, density of atomic hydrogen, and rate at which ultraviolet photons reach the molecule. A comparison of these theoretical population ratios with the observed ones then makes it possible to estimate these parameters. As it happens, under the conditions usually encountered, the temperature is not so important for these higher-$J$ levels. This is because the excitation energies of these levels much exceed the random thermal energies, collisional excitation becomes weak, and the chief effect of collisions is to de-excite states that have been excited by ultraviolet photon absorption; the rate at which this de-excitation occurs depends only weakly on the temperature.) So the comparison between theory and observation yields primarily the particle density of hydrogen and the intensity of ultraviolet radiation.

Such a comparison requires, of course, that we obtain values of the column density $N(J)$ for several excited rotational states, characterized by different values of $J$. As with the deuterium features, an empirical curve of growth must be used for this purpose. In this application, one problem appears that was not present for deuterium. For each excited $H_2$ rotational state, the $f$ values in the different bands range over a factor of ten. This range is sufficient to determine accurately a segment of the curve of growth but is often not enough to yield the full curve. To get around this problem, we assume that the same curve of growth applies to $H_2$ absorption features from all rotational levels. This plausible assumption seems to give self-consistent results for $N(J)$ in the lines of sight to most stars.

How this procedure works is shown in figure 6.3. In this plot the absorbed area, $W$, for each feature (see figure 4.1) is plotted against $Nf$; different symbols represent features due to absorption by $H_2$ molecules in four excited rotational states, $J = 3$ to $6$. Because of the large range in values of $Nf$, both $W$ and $Nf$ have been plotted on geometrical (or logarithmic) scales (see figure 5.2). The values of $f$ used are all known in advance (computed from theory). The values of $N$ assumed for each of the four different rotational states were those that gave the best fit of all the points with each other and with the solid, theoretical curve. This theoretical curve differs slightly from the one shown in figure 4.6 in that the average (rms) velocity spread, V, in the line of sight is different in the two figures—3.5 and 5 km sec⁻¹, respectively. As in figure 4.6, the small difference in wavelengths between different features has been ignored; the values given for the vertical and horizontal scales are based on a wavelength of 1,000 Å.

Examination of figure 5.3 reveals a number of interesting points. On the geometrical scale that is used, an increase in the assumed value of $N(J)$ moves the group of points for that $J$ to the right, without changing their relative positions within the group. Thus the process of finding an empirical curve of growth consists of sliding the four groups of points back and forth horizontally until they overlap as well as possible to give a single curve of growth, valid for all $J$. (No vertical shift is permitted in this process, since the values of $W$ are known definitely.) It may be seen that this process determines the ratios of the different $N(J)$ to each other. Whereas the group of points

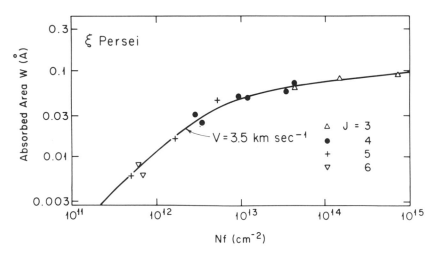

FIGURE 5.3 Curve of growth for $H_2$ in Xi Persei. The observed values of $W$, the absorbed area in each $H_2$ absorption feature, are plotted against $Nf$, where $f$ is the known oscillator strength for this feature. For each $J$, $N$ is the column density of $H_2$ molecules in the $J^{th}$ excited rotational state, with no vibrational or electronic excitation. The values of $N(J)$ for $J = 3, 4, 5$, and 6 were selected to give the best agreement between features of different $J$ and between all these features and the solid-line curve, computed theoretically for a velocity spread, $V$, equal to 3.5 km sec⁻¹ (rms).

for $J = 3$ in the figure might be moved to the right or left slightly, because they are on the flat section of the curve of growth, the groups of points for higher $J$ overlap well enough that there is little uncertainty in their relative N values. Fitting the theoretical curve to the final empirical one gives definite values for all N(J) and also determines V, the spread of velocities producing Doppler broadening. The small scatter of the points from the solid curve suggests that the column densities are determined rather accurately, except perhaps for N(3).

The resultant column densities for the different rotational levels have been used to determine n(H), the particle density of hydrogen atoms, and also the intensity of ultraviolet radiation. This last quantity can be expressed in terms of the average time an $H_2$ molecule must wait before it absorbs an ultraviolet photon; it is evident that the stronger the ultraviolet radiation, the shorter this photon absorption time will be. The results show that the most likely value of the photon absorption time is about 60 years. It is gratifying to find that this is about equal to the theoretical value for the average interstellar conditions within a few thousand light years of the Sun. The values of n(H) found for clouds showing this typical photon absorption time are mostly between 10 and 100 cm$^{-3}$, which is consistent with the data on the fraction of hydrogen in molecular form, plotted in figure 5.2. As a representative average density in such a cloud, we may take 40 atoms cm$^{-3}$.

One important result of this density determination is that it gives the thickness of a typical diffuse cloud. We saw in chapter 4 that N(H$_{Tot}$), the overall column density through such a cloud, averages about $4 \times 10^{20}$ cm$^{-2}$, about the same value found in chapter 2 from 21-cm studies. From the definition of column density, N(H) = L × n(H), where the particle density, n(H), is assumed to be constant over a length L and zero elsewhere. If we now set n(H) equal to 40 cm$^{-3}$, we find a value of $1 \times 10^{19}$ cm for L, or about 10 light years. Since cloud thicknesses cover a wide range of values, this result is certainly not applicable to all diffuse clouds, but it gives a useful estimate for a typical cloud. For a spherical cloud, an average thickness of 10 light years corresponds to a radius of about 7 light years, a value recently confirmed by direct measures based on the obscuration of stars at different distances. If all diffuse clouds are spheres of this radius, they must occupy about two percent of the volume of the galactic disc, in order to account for the total amount of cold gas observed in the disc.

A few of the clouds that show $H_2$ absorption and that have been studied with *Copernicus* show evidence of photon absorption times that are much shorter than the average value for interstellar gas in the galactic disc. For these clouds, the photon absorption times are in the range from about two to ten years. So intense an ultraviolet radiation field requires that these clouds be much closer to a hot star (which provides a good ultraviolet light source) than is the case for interstellar clouds generally. A typical distance of some 50 light years from such a star seems to be required. These particular clouds tend to have relatively high densities, between 100 and 1,000 atoms cm$^{-3}$, and have velocities away from the hot star toward the Earth of about 20 km sec$^{-1}$. Astronomers have believed for some time that the hydrogen gas near a hot star is ionized and heated and that, at the resulting high pressure, it expands rapidly into the surrounding cooler gas. The force of this expansion tends to compress even further any cool clouds in the neighborhood and to accelerate the clouds away from the star. Some such effect of violent activity near hot stars is presumably responsible for the high densities deduced from the *Copernicus* data. (Some of these denser clouds must be moving away from the Earth but will be beyond the hot star, where they produce no absorption features in the observed stellar spectrum.)

It seems remarkable that recording the number of photons reaching the Earth in a variety of wavelength bands should make it possible for us to find out how long, on the average, a hydrogen molecule within a cloud must wait before it absorbs a passing photon and is excited to a state of higher energy, or that further study will reveal how long the molecule must wait before it collides with a free atom. This first waiting time tells us how far the molecules are from the hot star that serves as a source of ultraviolet photons. The second waiting time tells us how many atoms (mostly hydrogen) are present in each cubic centimeter of the cloud.

## AN INTERSTELLAR CLOUD
## AS SEEN BY A CHEMIST

The study of chemistry is mostly a study of molecules—what holds them together, and how they are formed and destroyed. Research on the Universe outside our own solar system has in the past uncovered relatively little that is of interest to a chemist. While molecules are present in the atmospheres of cooler stars, an understanding of their formation presents no real challenge. In such atmospheres, molecules form and dissociate rapidly and are in *thermal equilibrium* with the gas and the radiation, which are at about the same temperature. Under these conditions, the population ratios of molecules and atoms of different types may be found directly from the well-known binding energy of each molecule.

Research within the last decade has shown that molecules are abundant not only in cool stellar atmospheres but also in some interstellar clouds, especially those whose density is higher than average. Evidence from microwave studies, showing the importance of molecules in such clouds, will be discussed in the next chapter. Interstellar clouds are generally far from thermal equilibrium. (In particular the amount of radiant energy present is enormously less than would be found under equilibrium conditions at the gas temperature.) Hence the fraction of atoms bound in molecules between the stars depends on the specific chemical reactions occurring. Molecular hydrogen plays a dominant part in these reactions, which are, therefore, discussed in this chapter.

A significant characteristic of $H_2$ molecules is that they can interact with atoms to form molecules of a quite different type. One important such reaction is the following:

$$H_2 + O^+ \rightarrow HO^+ + H. \qquad (1)$$

This expression tells us that an oxygen atom which is missing one electron, and is therefore positively charged, can collide with an $H_2$ molecule and change places with one of the two hydrogen atoms. The neutral hydrogen atom displaced by the $O^+$ ion then goes away, carrying off the energy released in this exchange reaction. (We use HO here, instead of the chemists' more usual symbol, OH, to agree with the designation of the water molecule as $H_2O$.)

The $HO^+$ molecule produced in reaction (1) can collide with two $H_2$ molecules in succession, producing the following reactions:

$$H_2 + HO^+ \rightarrow H_2O^+ + H \qquad (2)$$

and

$$H_2 + H_2O^+ \rightarrow H_3O^+ + H. \qquad (3)$$

Evidently a hydrogen atom prefers the company of an oxygen ion, even with several hydrogen atoms attached, to the company of its own kind. Finally a free electron combines with the $H_3O^+$ molecule, forming a familiar water molecule ($H_2O$) according to the following reaction:

$$H_3O^+ + e^- \rightarrow H_2O + H. \qquad (4)$$

In this sequence of reactions, three hydrogen molecules have reacted with one oxygen ion and one electron, forming one $H_2O$ molecule and dissociating two $H_2$ molecules into four hydrogen atoms. This reaction chain is believed to be the primary source of the $H_2O$ molecules observed between the stars.

The reaction chains involved in the formation of other molecules are more complex, but the types of reactions are similar, often involving a rearrangement of partners in two colliding molecules or dissociation of a molecular ion following electron capture. Photon absorption, producing molecular dissociation, is also important and is one of several processes that can destroy the $H_2O$ molecules formed in reaction (4) above. Detailed calculations of all these processes, and others also, can explain in a general way the abundances of most interstellar molecules involving the heavy elements carbon, nitrogen, oxygen, magnesium, silicon, sulphur, and iron. The importance of $H_2$ is indicated by the fact that such abundant molecules as carbon monoxide (CO) and oxygen ($O_2$) tend to form from molecules produced by $H_2$, such as HCO and HO. The relative abundances found from these theoretical calculations are mostly in rough agreement with the observations discussed in the next chapter, although many uncertainties remain.

A major discrepancy between this theory and the observations relates to $CH^+$, whose abundance relative to H and CH is observed to be several hundred times greater than the theory predicts. The difficulty is that while reactions similar to reaction (1) take place when many other types of atomic ions are substituted for $O^+$, such a reaction fails to work for $C^+$. In fact, for $C^+$ the reaction goes the other way; evidently a neutral hydrogen atom finds a $C^+$ ion a somewhat unattractive partner and prefers its own kind when faced with a choice. Hence a neutral hydrogen atom will displace the $C^+$ ion from a $CH^+$ molecule, the two hydrogen atoms sticking together to form an $H_2$ molecule. Perhaps, as some astronomers have suggested, $CH^+$ is formed in gas that has been transiently heated; if the $H_2$ molecule has sufficient energy, it will sometimes form a $CH^+$ molecule when it collides with $C^+$. Alternatively, an appreciable number of carbon-carrying molecules could form on dust grains, just as $H_2$ is formed.

The mechanisms of molecule formation and disruption in interstellar clouds provide challenging problems in chemistry. Attempts to explain theoretically the observed molecular abundances are promising enough to suggest that we are on the right track but these same theories also raise questions and stimulate further research. This state of affairs is typical of new and exciting scientific fields.

## SUMMARY

The fraction of hydrogen in molecular form is radically different for different values of the overall hydrogen column density, with only about one molecule per $10^5$ hydrogen atoms in thin, relatively transparent clouds (with $N(H_{Tot})$ less than $10^{20}$ cm$^{-2}$) but with much of the hydrogen in molecular form in thick, heavily obscuring clouds (with $N(H_{Tot})$ exceeding $10^{21}$ cm$^{-2}$). This result agrees with theoretical computations, which show that within the thick obscuring clouds, absorption by an outer shell of $H_2$ molecules shields the inner molecules from the ultraviolet radiation that could dissociate them.

Measurements of the population ratios for rotationally excited states in $H_2$ molecules show that the temperature within a typical diffuse cloud is about 80° K. The density within such a cloud is generally in the range from 10 to 100 hydrogen atoms cm$^{-3}$. In some clouds the column densities of molecules in rotationally excited states indicate that the density is some tenfold higher than this and that the ultraviolet radiation is more intense than normal, presumably because the cloud is relatively close to a hot star.

A typical average density of 40 hydrogen atoms cm$^{-3}$, combined with the average column density of $4 \times 10^{20}$ cm$^{-3}$, determined earlier for a diffuse cloud, gives a typical thickness of about 10 light years for such a cloud. About two percent of the volume of the galactic disc is occupied by these cool clouds.

Reactions of $H_2$ molecules with heavy atoms dominate the chemistry of the interstellar material, accounting for the formation of many of the molecules that are observed.

# 6

# Heavy Elements Between the Stars

The overwhelming abundance of hydrogen and helium throughout the Universe has been emphasized in earlier chapters. All other elements are present only as traces, both in the interstellar medium and in most stars. According to table 1.1, carbon and oxygen together amount to one atom for every 1,000 hydrogen atoms. All the other heavy elements add up to only about one in 3,000.

If these impurities were not present at all, the Universe would be a much simpler place, devoid of the air, water, fire, and life so evident here on Earth. Between the stars also, heavy elements, though relatively scarce, are involved in an enormous variety of processes, which affect the overall behavior and evolution of the interstellar gas. In addition, they provide us with important clues as to just what is going on between the stars; in particular, they can be used to find the temperature and density, as well as the chemical composition, of the gas.

In this chapter we discuss the clues that have been discovered recently. First, we shall see how *Copernicus* data on ultraviolet absorption features, together with X-ray measurements, have led to the discovery of a hot phase in the interstellar gas, with a temperature of about a million degrees. Next, we shall consider the information available on the chemical composition of the gas, as deduced primarily from absorption features at ultraviolet wavelengths; these data indicate that most atoms of certain elements have condensed on solid dust grains. Finally, we shall discuss the new information provided by microwave observations of molecular emission features, confirming the relatively high density and low temperature of the molecular clouds.

We summarize here, in passing, some new information on dust grains, which was obtained during the decade 1970–80, and which

**118**

is a substantial addition to the information presented in chapter 2. Ultraviolet observations made with a relatively wide measurement band, particularly by the University of Wisconsin instruments on the OAO-2 satellite, have shown that a variety of different types of grains are present between the stars. Some of these solid particles have very small dimensions, perhaps as small as a few hundred Ångstroms. In particular, a strong absorption feature some 300 Å wide, centered at 2,200 Å, has been attributed to tiny particles of carbon in the form of graphite. Infrared telescopes flying above much of the atmosphere have observed the emission of radiation from interstellar grains. Many newly formed stars are surrounded by obscuring clouds, in which most of the stellar radiation is absorbed by grains and re-emitted in the far infrared.

## THE CORONAL GAS

The discovery of the coronal gas began in 1956 in the course of an observational program by G. Münch on interstellar $Ca^+$ absorption features. He measured these features in stars at a variety of distances from the galactic plane; as in figure 2.5, the absorption spectrum for each line of sight showed a number of separate features. Each such feature, called a component of the $Ca^+$ interstellar absorption, is at-tributed to a separate cloud; as we have seen in chapter 2, the sepa-rate components have different wavelengths because of different ve-locities of the individual clouds, again a result of the Doppler effect. Münch found that the number of interstellar $Ca^+$ components ob-served in the spectrum of a star increased with increasing stellar dis-tance, even for stars several thousand light years above the galactic plane. This result could be explained by assuming that some of the absorbing clouds were also at distances of a few thousand light years from the mid-plane of the Galaxy. Since the distance from the ga-lactic plane is usually denoted by $z$, these clouds are referred to as high-z objects.

A separate analysis showed that the existence of such high-z clouds posed an interesting theoretical problem. The mass of the ga-lactic disc is large, and its gravitational attraction tends to pull all matter toward it. For this reason, stars in the galactic disc can rise as much as several thousand light years above the mid-plane of the disc only if they have very high velocities. There are relatively few stars at such distances, and, as far as we can tell, there is relatively little gas and dust. The high-z clouds are unusual objects and must have had high velocities (perhaps a hundred kilometers per second) when

they were near the mid-plane some $10^7$ years ago. This result, by itself, was not too surprising, since clouds with this velocity had been
known before.

A more difficult problem is how the clouds can exist as separate
entities. Gas has a tendency to expand, and to hold a gaseous aggregation together requires some sort of force. In astronomical situations, the two chief forces that can confine a cloud of gas are gravi-
tation and external pressure. The self-gravitational force of a typical
diffuse cloud, as observed in absorption (by dust or hydrogen or
heavy atoms), is inadequate for this purpose. To hold a diffuse cloud
together requires the pressure of a surrounding gas permeating the
space between clouds and sometimes called an *intercloud medium*.
Thirty years ago theorists had hypothesized that such a medium per-
meated the galatic disc, with a pressure about equal to that in the
diffuse clouds. This assumption provided the external pressure
needed to explain the continued existence of diffuse clouds.

However, this assumption had to be reconciled with the observation that the intercloud medium, in contrast to the diffuse clouds,
produces no strong absorption of starlight and hence is difficult to
observe directly. This reconciliation follows directly if one assumes
that the temperature of this medium is much higher than that of the
diffuse clouds. It is a well-known physical law that the pressure, $p$,
within a gas is proportional to the product of the particle density, $n$,
and the temperature, $T$. (Quantitatively, $p = nkT$, where $k$ is the gas
constant.) It follows that if the temperature in an intercloud medium
is a hundred times that in a diffuse cloud, the particle density
needed to produce the same pressure is only one-hundredth as great.
The 21-cm data had earlier suggested a temperature of 100° K for the
cool clouds; a temperature of 10,000° K for the intercloud medium
seemed not unreasonable, giving a plausibly low density for this
medium.

The difficulty with this picture, as far as the high-z clouds are
concerned, is that an intercloud medium at 10,000° K would tend to
be confined to the galactic disc and would have a negligible density
and pressure a few thousand light years from the disc. A similar effect occurs in the Earth's atmosphere. The average vertical velocity
of a nitrogen molecule (at 0°C) is about 0.4 km sec[-1], enough to carry
the molecule up to a height of 8 km (about the altitude of Mt. Ever-
est). At greater heights the air density is much reduced. For interstellar gas to reach the position of Münch's high-z clouds, a few
thousand light years from the galactic plane, requires a vertical velocity in the plane of 100 km sec[-1], ten times higher than the random

thermal speed of about 10 km sec$^{-1}$ for hydrogen at 10,000° K. To give hydrogen atoms an average random velocity of 100 km sec$^{-1}$ requires a temperature of $10^{6°}$ K.

To a theorist, the existence of the high-z clouds seemed an indirect, but nevertheless persuasive, argument that an intercloud medium must be present, extending far from the galactic disc, and it seemed necessary to assume a high temperature for such a distant or tension of the gas. This hypothetical, million-degree medium was named a *galactic corona*, by analogy with the solar corona, which is an envelope of hot gas, also at about $10^{6°}$ K, surrounding the Sun and extending far above the solar surface. The density of gas in the solar corona, while very low by terrestrial standards, is high enough that this gas radiates weakly at a variety of wavelengths. The galactic corona, on the other hand, has such a low density that it would not be expected to produce any appreciable emission or absorption of visible light or radio waves. Hence in 1956 its existence could not be confirmed directly.

If such a corona were composed of pure hydrogen at a temperature of $10^{6°}$ K, all the atoms would be fully ionized, and, in the absence of orbital electrons, no absorption or emission features could be produced. Weak emission of soft X-rays with a featureless, or continuous, spectrum would provide the only practical method of detecting such a corona by means of electromagnetic radiation. Heavy atoms in such a hot gas would be more easily detected, however, since many of them would still have a few electrons bound in orbit around the nucleus. For example, oxygen atoms, which have eight orbital electrons in the neutral state, will usually have from one to three bound electrons in the corona at a gas temperature of $10^{6°}$ K. These atoms can absorb ultraviolet light. In particular, the $O^{+5}$ atom has two strong absorption features at 1,032 and 1,038 Å (as well as X-ray features at energies of about a hundred electron Volts). One of the principal objectives of the Princeton telescope-spectrometer on *Copernicus* was to look for these $O^{+5}$ absorption features produced by hot coronal gas in the Galaxy. Sensitivity at wavelengths shorter than 1,150 Å, achieved with considerable difficulty, was clearly mandatory for this research.

To our gratification, most of the hot stars observed with *Copernicus* did show these features. Sample data are given in figure 6.1, which shows a plot of an $O^{+5}$ absorption feature in Alpha Virginis (also called Spica and one of the twenty brightest stars in the sky). Plots for two other interstellar features in the same star are shown for comparison. The $O^{+5}$ feature (which is somewhat narrower in Alpha

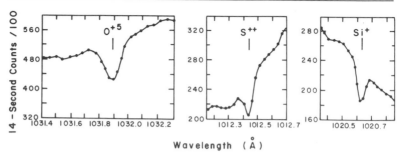

FIGURE 6.1 Profiles of absorption features in Alpha Virginis. The 14-second photon counts are plotted against wavelength for three absorption features. For each feature, a vertical line again indicates the central wavelength.

Virginis than in most other stars) is at least twice as wide as the other two interstellar features. This great width is unique for weak interstellar features. (Strong, saturated features can be wide, as evidenced by the winged $H_2$ features in figure 5.1.) If the observed $O^{+5}$ widths are attributed to random thermal velocities, the temperature of the coronal gas responsible for the $O^{+5}$ absorption is about $10^{6°}$ K, with values for individual lines of sight ranging from about half to twice this value. A temperature of this order is about what had been predicted several decades earlier.

Values of the temperature determined from line widths represent upper limits, since large-scale motions in the gas may account for some of the velocity spread along the line of sight. Indeed, a detailed analysis of the data obtained for some seventy stars, all but eight of which showed measurable $O^{+5}$ absorption, indicates that each absorption feature is composed of several components. A lower limit of $0.2 \times 10^{6°}$ K for the gas temperature is obtained from the weakness of the comparable $N^{+4}$ absorption features at 1,239 and 1,243 Å. At temperatures of at least this amount, most nitrogen atoms will have lost at least five bound electrons as a result of collisions with electrons; it is for this reason that relatively few $N^{+4}$ ionized atoms are present. Similar results are obtained from $S^{+3}$ and $Si^{+3}$ absorption features.

A coronal temperature of roughly a million degrees in order of magnitude seems clearly demonstrated. We shall refer to a gas at this temperature as "hot." The ionized regions that surround luminous young stars, whose temperature is about 8,000° K, will be referred to as "warm,"—a useful distinction, though perhaps a slight perversion of the English language! (By comparison, the temperatures of stellar atmospheres mostly range from 3,000 to 30,000° K, while the temperature of the cold diffuse interstellar clouds is about 80° K.)

The highly ionized heavy atoms in the hot coronal gas should emit X-rays with energies up to a few hundred electron Volts. Many closely spaced emission features would be expected in the soft X-ray spectrum. As we saw at the end of chapter 2, a general field of soft X-rays reaching the Earth from all over the sky was detected in the 1960s. Related measurements of hard X-rays reaching the Earth had shown that these more energetic photons were produced largely by individual sources. As a result, X-ray astronomers were naturally inclined to expect a similar explanation for soft X-rays. In the long run, our scientific theories are controlled by "hard, stubborn" facts. However in those areas where research is still in progress and most "facts" are a bit uncertain, the working hypotheses that scientists make to help understand the data will naturally depend on the existing climate of opinion.

The University of Wisconsin X-ray detector flown with Skylab (see chapter 3) was designed to search for point sources of soft X-rays, and, in particular, to measure the intensity of such radiation from known stars. Although the field of view ($2°$ by $20°$) was not very small, any bright point source could have been detected as the telescope scanned across it. About one tenth of the sky was surveyed. As noted earlier, no point sources were seen with either this or other instruments, yielding rather low upper limits on the soft X-ray emissivity of various types of stars. These results, taken together with the $O^{+5}$ absorption measures, leave little doubt that these X-rays must be produced by a hot intercloud medium between the stars.

More detailed analysis of X-ray data indicates that no one temperature will fit the observations. Whereas the measurement band for soft X-rays has not been narrow enough to show individual emission features, broad-band measures give the shape of the smoothed spectrum. To explain this spectrum, it is necessary to assume that the soft X-rays are produced in regions at several different temperatures, some greater than $10^{6°}$ K, others less. For example, two types of coronal gas, one at $3 \times 10^{6°}$ K, the other at $6 \times 10^{5°}$ K, will satisfy the X-ray data. According to this theory the absorbing $O^{+5}$ ions are almost all in the cooler regions, since in the hotter regions the oxygen atoms are almost entirely stripped of their electrons. The pressure found for these regions is some two to three times higher than the average value found for diffuse clouds in chapter 5, though this result is somewhat uncertain observationally.

As we shall see in the next chapter, the coronal gas is probably maintained by the explosive force of supernova remnants, propagating through and around the dense clouds of neutral hydrogen. In this picture, a substantial variety of temperatures within this very hot gas is to be expected. In particular, a reduced coronal temperature near cold, dense clouds is expected theoretically (see chapter 7). In addition, some excess of pressure of the exploding gas over the pressure in the diffuse clouds, as suggested by the observations, seems physically plausible.

## ABUNDANCES AND TEMPERATURE WITHIN DIFFUSE CLOUDS

The *Copernicus* instrument has made it possible to measure the relative numbers of atoms of many chemical elements in the interstellar gas. The methods described at the beginning of chapter 4 have been used to determine column densities of various heavy elements. For an element of type X, we divide $N(X_{Tot})$—the column density for atoms of element X, including those in all stages of ionization as well as in molecules—by $N(H_{Tot})$—the corresponding overall column density of hydrogen along the same line of sight—to obtain the abundance of element X relative to hydrogen. It is customary to express these results in terms of cosmic abundances, shown for the ten most abundant elements in table 1.1.

For this purpose the *depletion factor* is introduced; for an element, X, the depletion factor is defined as the ratio of the relative abundance measured in the interstellar gas (equal to $[N(X_{Tot})/N(H_{Tot})]$) to the cosmic relative abundance (equal to $[N(X_{Tot})/N(H_{Tot})]_{cosmic}$). Thus, if the abundance of an element relative to hydrogen in the interstellar gas just equals the cosmic value (that is, there is no depletion), the depletion factor for that element equals 1. If the interstellar abundance relative to hydrogen is only one percent of its cosmic value, then the depletion factor is 0.01.

The most complete abundance measures are those for the line of sight to Zeta Ophiuchi, a rather bright star that is appreciably reddened, indicating that the line of sight passes through a substantial amount of dust and hence of gas. Quantitatively, $N(H_{Tot})$ for this star is about $1.4 \times 10^{21}$ $cm^{-2}$, of which about two-thirds is in molecular form; this column density is about four times that for an average diffuse cloud. The hydrogen particle density within the Zeta Ophiuchi cloud is at least 200 atoms $cm^{-3}$, exceeding the values for more typical diffuse clouds.

Values of the depletion factors for nineteen elements, in the Zeta

Ophiuchi clouds, plus upper limits for five more, are shown in figure 6.2. The vertical axis makes use of a geometrical (or logarithmic) scale, as in figures 5.2 and 5.3. The horizontal scale is a computed *condensation temperature* for each element. This is the temperature at which an element in the gas will condense into solid particles. This temperature is computed on the assumption that the density is high enough that molecules are frequently formed and destroyed, and that the resultant abundances of different molecules are those in thermal equilibrium. As we saw in chapter 5, this assumption of

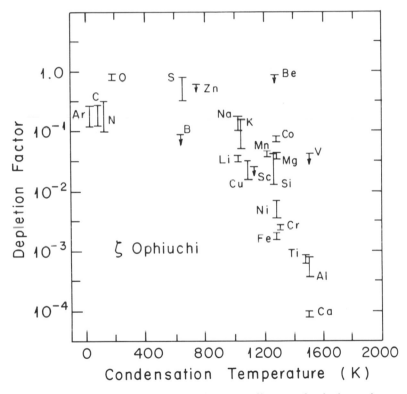

FIGURE 6.2 Depletion of elements in the interstellar gas. The depletion factor for different elements is shown for the gas clouds between the Earth and Zeta Ophiuchi. For each element the value of the depletion factor (the abundance relative to hydrogen divided by the corresponding cosmic abundance relative to hydrogen) is plotted against the temperature at which that element will condense into solid particles.

thermal equilibrium is a good one for stellar atmospheres, where the densities exceed those in diffuse clouds by an enormous factor, and where the radiation temperatures do not differ much from the gas temperatures. This assumption is definitely unrealistic for the diffuse interstellar clouds. Nevertheless, the computed condensation temperatures should give some indication of the relative condensability of different elements in such clouds.

The abundances of fourteen of these nineteen elements were determined from *Copernicus* observations, which yielded column densities for elements in their dominant stage of ionization, and often in one or more other stages of ionization as well. In this way values of $N(X_{Tot})$, the column density summed over all stages of ionization, could be obtained directly. The remaining five elements were measured from the ground, but in only one case (titanium) did ground measurements give the column density of an element in its most abundant stage of ionization ($Ti^+$). For the other four elements, the measures gave column densities of neutral atoms (or of $Ca^+$), and large corrections had to be applied to obtain the abundances of the dominant singly ionized atoms (or of $Ca^{++}$). Thanks to *Copernicus* observations of such ratios as $N(C)/N(C^+)$ and $N(Mg)/N(Mg^+)$, and also to the ground-based determination of $N(Ca)/N(Ca^+)$, these corrections could be made with some, if not complete, confidence.

The vertical bars in figure 6.2 show estimated ranges of values consistent with known sources of possible error. For strong features, appreciable errors may result from problems associated with the use of the curve of growth, especially when several clouds are present along the line of sight, as is known to be the case for Zeta Ophiuchi. The very short vertical bars represent mainly those elements for which accurate measures were obtained on relatively weak absorption features, which seemed safely on the proportional section of the curve of growth. For the element oxygen (at a condensation temperature of about 200° K), the column density was determined from the relatively weak, but measurable, wings of the very strong absorption feature at 1,302 Å. There is some question as to whether the depletions of argon (Ar), carbon (C), and nitrogen (N) are as great as shown in the figure.

The general trend shown in figure 6.2 strongly suggests that the depletion observed for some interstellar elements results from condensation on grains. The good agreement between the mass available in condensable elements and the mass required for the observed interstellar dust, which was noted in chapter 2, provides strong confirmation of this viewpoint. Most grains are probably composed of such familiar minerals as enstatite—$(Fe, Mg)SiO_3$—and olivine—$(Fe, Mg)_2$

$SiO_4$; magnesium, iron, and silicon, whose oxides make up these minerals, are the only strongly depleted among the ten most abundant ones (see table 1.1).

Although the observed depletions seem to be in general agreement with grain formation, it seems unlikely that the interstellar grains have formed under the conditions assumed in computing the condensation temperature. The actual process is doubtless much more complicated. For example, the element carbon has a very low computed condensation temperature, since for the equilibrium conditions assumed in the calculations, nearly all carbon atoms are assumed bound to oxygen to form carbon monoxide. In fact, many carbon atoms in interstellar clouds are likely to stick together to form graphite, which condenses at a very high temperature. As noted at the beginning of this chapter, ultraviolet measures of grain absorption actually indicate that tiny graphite particles may be important constituents of the interstellar dust. The detailed analysis of the processes by which interstellar atoms stick together to form grains and of the resulting structure within the grains should be a challenging task for the future.

The variation in depletion from one cloud to another can provide important information on the formative and destructive processes that influence the amount of material in dust grains. The most striking result is that the depletion tends to diminish with increasing cloud velocity. Even for a velocity of about 15 km sec$^{-1}$, the depletion factors for calcium, magnesium, silicon, and iron are appreciably closer to unity than they are in clouds with a velocity of at most 5 km sec$^{-1}$. In clouds with a velocity as great as 100 km sec$^{-1}$, the abundances appear close to cosmic, with depletion factors equal to about one. This result can be easily understood if we assume that the same process that accelerates the cloud tends at the same time to destroy the grains. This assumption is plausible, since most acceleration processes will act primarily on the atoms, which will then collide at high velocities with the grains. Such atom-grain collisions will tend to knock atoms out of the grains (a process known as *sputtering*) and will reduce the amount of material in solid form.

This conclusion, that in high-velocity clouds grains have somehow been converted back to gas, reducing the depletion, had been suggested very tentatively as early as 1954. Such a hypothesis offered one way of explaining how the Na and Ca$^+$ absorption features varied with cloud velocity. However, it was the recent, broad investigation of interstellar depletion, led by the *Copernicus* program, that firmly established this result.

Systematic surveys of interstellar iron features (from *Copernicus*)

and interstellar titanium features (from the ground) suggest that depletions are smaller for lines of sight along which the average density
of the gas is appreciably lower than its typical value in diffuse
clouds. This result may be due to a slower growth of grains in gas of
lower density, or perhaps to a greater tendency of these low-density
regions to be accelerated occasionally to transient states of high velocity, destroying many of the grains.

We turn now to the use of absorption features as probes of physical conditions in the interstellar gas. The simplest application of
this sort is to use the random radial velocities of absorbing atoms to
yield the gas temperature. As we have seen (pp. 93, 112), the quantity $V$, defined as the (rms) spread of radial velocities (sometimes
called the velocity dispersion), may be obtained from the curve of
growth. One complication is that large-scale motions in the gas can
produce a spread of velocities entirely unrelated to temperature. Fortunately this latter spread of velocities should be the same for atoms
of all elements, while the thermal spread is less for the heavier atoms; in thermal motion, the product of the atomic weight, $A$, and the
square of the random velocity, $V$, should have the same average
value for all atoms (Quantitatively, $V^2 = kT/Am_0$, where $m_0$ is the
mass of unit atomic weight, and $k$ is again the gas constant.) Hence
these two effects can be distinguished if we have results on $V$ for atoms of widely different values of $A$.

Observational results of this sort are plotted in figure 6.3, obtained for ultraviolet absorption features in Alpha Virginis (Spica),
for which data were presented also in figure 6.1. For each absorption
feature, we measure the velocities of the absorbing atoms with respect to those that absorb at the center of the feature; then $V$ is the
average (rms) velocity spread of all the atoms producing that particular feature. As in figure 4.6, $V$ is determined from the curve of
growth for the features absorbed by that particular type of atom. The
circles in figure 6.3 represent the observed values of $V^2$, in
(km sec$^{-1}$)$^2$, plotted against $1/A$ for different elements. The straight
dashed line in the figure represents the theoretical result for a gas
temperature of 7,500° K. Evidently this line provides a good fit to the
data, indicating an actual temperature of about 7,500° K for this gas
of predominantly neutral hydrogen.

This result is in sharp contrast to the temperature of 80° K found
for a typical diffuse cloud, with a hydrogen column density of $4 \times$
$10^{20}$ cm$^{-2}$. Clearly, there is much less gas in the line of sight to Alpha
Virginis; the column density of neutral hydrogen is only $10^{19}$ cm$^{-2}$.
Since the distance of the star is about 300 light years, the mean hy-

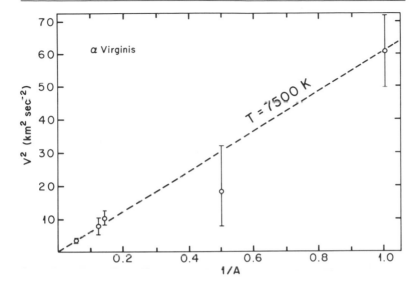

FIGURE 6.3 Velocity spread for different elements. The circles represent different values of $V^2$ obtained from curves of growth for interstellar absorption features produced by different elements with different values of the atomic weight, $A$, along the line of sight to Alpha Virginis. The vertical bars show estimated (rms) observational errors.

drogen density is about 0.04 cm$^{-3}$, a very low value. (The relatively small distance from the Sun minimizes the curve-of-growth complications resulting from the presence of many different clouds along the line of sight.) We have seen in chapter 2 that comparison of hydrogen absorption and emission at 21 cm wavelength showed that some regions were cold—about 80° K—and some were warm—more than 1,000° K. Copernicus measures have now confirmed the existence of the warm neutral gas as well as the cold gas, and have given a specific value for the temperature. Interstellar features in several other stars near the Sun have yielded similarly high values for the temperature in clouds with relatively low $N(H_{Tot})$ and correspondingly low reddening by dust.

## MOLECULES IN DENSER CLOUDS

The presence of some molecules in interstellar space has been known for many years. The molecules CH and CN, as well as the ionized molecule CH$^+$, produce absorption features in visible light. Their presence in diffuse clouds has been known since the early 1940s, when these interstellar features were first identified in the spectra of several stars. Only a very small fraction of interstellar carbon and nitrogen atoms (less than $10^{-4}$) are bound in these molecules.

It was not until the advent of radio astronomy that features from a wide variety of molecules in interstellar space were discovered. First to be found in this way, in 1963, was a pair of absorption features produced by the HO molecule at wavelength of about 18 cm. Five years later, interstellar emission was detected at 1.26 cm from the familiar ammonia molecule ($NH_3$). In 1969 the formaldehyde molecule ($H_2CO$) was detected at 6.2 cm, again in absorption rather than emission.

During the 1970s many more types of molecules have been detected by their emission features at radio wavelengths, mostly in the microwave region—at wavelengths below 10 cm (see figure 3.1). Some fifty different molecules have now been detected, many of them organic molecules built around carbon atoms; some of these complex structures contain as many as nine to eleven atoms. Of all the molecules observed in interstellar space to date, water ($H_2O$) and alcohol (more properly, ethyl alcohol—$C_2H_5OH$) are the most familiar. Hydrogen cyanide (HCN) and carbon monoxide (CO) are among the poisonous gases detected between the stars.

A very large number of distinct emission features have been observed from these interstellar molecules, with about a dozen features for each molecule on the average. In the important carbon monoxide molecule, for example, each transition between excited rotational states produces an emission feature. The transition from the first excited state ($J = 1$) down to the ground state ($J = 0$) produces a feature at 0.26 cm. Other interstellar absorption features are produced by transitions from the second to the first excited rotational states (from $J = 2$ to $J = 1$), giving photons with a wavelength of 0.13 cm, and from the third down to the second (from $J = 3$ to $J = 2$), with a wavelength of 0.087 cm. Moreover, different features, with somewhat different wavelengths, are produced when a rare heavy isotope of carbon (with an atomic weight, $A$, of 13 instead of 12) or of oxygen (with $A = 18$ instead of 16) is substituted in the molecule. (These two types of molecules are designated $^{13}CO$ and $C^{18}O$; we omit the superscripts 12 and 16 for the abundant isotopes of C and O, respectively.)

This large number of features produced by molecules of one type is highly useful if the intensity of radiation from these molecules is to be used as a probe of physical conditions within interstellar clouds. On the simplest possible model, each cloud may be assumed homogeneous, with the gas temperature, $T$, assumed to be constant throughout the cloud. Also, in this idealized model, we assume that the molecules are excited from the ground state by collisions with the predominant hydrogen molecules, whose particle density, $n(H_2)$, is also assumed constant. The intensity of radiation emitted in the CO emission feature, for example, will depend on the column density of CO, $N(CO)$, along the line of sight through the cloud as well as on $n(H_2)$ and $T$ within the cloud, and can be computed for this simple model. Fitting the model to the observations then requires adjusting three quantities, $N(CO)$, $n(H_2)$, and $T$ to give the best agreement. To determine all three quantities separately requires measurements of at least three emission features. However, our confidence in the results will be boosted if many more such features can be measured, and if any group of three gives the same values for $N(CO)$, $n(H_2)$, and $T$.

This situation is similar, in principle, to the use of $H_2$ absorption features as probes of diffuse clouds, a technique discussed in the previous chapter. There, values of $N(J)$, the $H_2$ column density for the $J^{th}$ excited rotational level, were obtained for a variety of $J$ values (between four and six for the lines of sight to most stars) and were used to determine two or three physical quantities within the clouds.

While the use of molecular emission features as probes of interstellar clouds is straightforward in theory, in practice it is complicated by a number of factors that diminish somewhat the accuracy and reliability of the results. We have seen in previous chapters how the interpretation of absorption features is complicated by the phenomenon of saturation—that is, when the column density of absorbing atoms becomes too large, all the photons within a certain wavelength band are absorbed, and observation of the absorption feature gives only a lower limit for the column density. A similar phenomenon appears with emission. If the column density of some molecule is relatively large, the photons emitted by molecules of this type will be absorbed by other identical molecules; the emission feature is then said to be self-absorbed and gives only a lower limit for the column density. The 0.26-cm emission feature of interstellar CO is almost always self-absorbed, and observations of the much weaker isotopic molecules ($^{13}CO$ or $C^{18}O$) are of great importance.

Another serious complication results from the fact that the rate at which an upper state is excited depends on transitions to that state from a variety of other states. Some of these transitions involve the absorption of radiation; to compute the transition rates, the particle density of photons, most of which have been emitted from excited molecules in the cloud, must be known. Thus, excitation of molecules at some point in the cloud depends on excitation all through the cloud. Such (integral) equations are well known in science, but their solution is often difficult. This intricate problem does not arise in the analysis of absorption features at ultraviolet or visible wavelengths, because the number of absorbing atoms is usually not much affected by the intensity of the radiation being absorbed. In the analysis of molecular emission features, these various problems have been circumvented by means of suitable approximations and assumptions. The values obtained for molecular column densities, temperatures, and $H_2$ particle densities are results of major significance but could well be incorrect by factors of two or so.

The results indicate that, in general, the gas showing strong molecular features is very much denser than the gas in a diffuse cloud, though still an almost perfect vacuum by terrestrial standards. Typical values of $n(H_2)$ range from about $10^2$ cm$^{-3}$ for clouds showing CO, up to values between $10^4$ and $10^6$ cm$^{-3}$ for clouds showing strong features from many molecules. By comparison, within most diffuse clouds $n(H_2)$ is in the range from 10 to 100 cm$^{-3}$, as we have seen in the previous chapter. The molecular clouds are also somewhat cooler than the diffuse clouds, with $T$ mostly between 20 and 50° K for the former, as compared to the average value of 80° K for the latter.

In addition, the total amount of material in the line of sight through a molecular cloud is generally much greater than that through a diffuse cloud, with $N(H_{Tot})$, the overall column density of hydrogen (atomic plus molecular) exceeding $10^{22}$ cm$^{-2}$, ten to a hundred times that in a typical diffuse cloud (see figure 5.2). Since the dust and gas increase together, it follows that a typical molecular cloud is highly opaque; few stars can be seen through such a cloud, and the inside is almost entirely shielded against ultraviolet radiation by the outer layers of dust. For building up a high concentration of molecules, shielding against the ultraviolet light that would dissociate them is fully as important as the higher density and lower temperature that encourage molecule formation.

Measures of the column densities for different types of molecules indicate that after $H_2$, CO is overwhelmingly the most abundant molecule. In molecular clouds the abundance ratio $N(CO)/N(H_{Tot})$ of carbon monoxide molecules to hydrogen atoms, mostly in $H_2$ molecules, is between $10^{-4}$ and $10^{-5}$. If we take $3 \times 10^{-5}$ as a typical value for this ratio, the cosmic abundances in table 1.1 show that about ten percent of the carbon atoms are tied up in CO molecules. The un-observed molecules $O_2$ and $N_2$ may also be abundant, but the relative numbers of most other molecules are much less. As noted at the end of the previous chapter, the theory of how these molecules form from $H_2$ reproduces roughly most of the observed abundances. One of the chief uncertainties in these calculations is the depletion; the abun-dances of different elements in the gaseous phase (not locked up in the grains) determine in turn the abundances of the different mole-cules in the gas.

A major finding of microwave studies is that the gas responsible for molecular emission shows some concentration in large clouds, each with an extent of some 200 light years. These giant molecular clouds, as they are often called, are very inhomogeneous, containing dense cores separated by gas of lower density; they should be re-garded, perhaps, as cloud complexes rather than clouds. Measurable CO emission is produced throughout these aggregations. Emission from other molecules is produced in the dense cores. The mass of one of these cloud complexes typically exceeds $10^5$ solar masses and may well be nearer to $10^6$ solar masses.

Detailed surveys of these giant molecular clouds have been made with telescopes sensitive to the 0.26-cm CO emission feature. Most such clouds are appreciably nearer to the center of the Galaxy than we are. Bright young stars, which have formed relatively recently, have a distribution in the Galaxy very similar to that of the molecular clouds, suggesting that star formation occurs in such clouds. In fact, many of these giant clouds are relatively close (a light year or less) to clusters of bright, young stars. One of the nearest giant molecular clouds, that in the constellation Orion, is adjacent to the Orion neb-ula (see p. 46), which surrounds a group of young stars (including the four closely spaced stars that constitute the Trapezium). All these stars must have formed within the last few million years, probably out of cold, dense gas that was then part of the molecular cloud. Fur-ther details of star formation in this region are discussed in the final chapter, together with the relationships between such regions and other kinds of regions in interstellar space.


## SUMMARY

During the decade 1970–80, radiation emitted or absorbed by the heavy elements has been measured by the ultraviolet telescope-spec-trometer on *Copernicus*, by X-ray telescopes above the atmosphere, and by microwave radio telescopes on the ground, with the following results.

The widespread presence of oxygen atoms ionized five times ($O^{+5}$), as indicated by ultraviolet interstellar absorption features in most stellar spectra, together with the soft X-rays received from most regions of the sky, show that a hot gas at a temperature of about a million degrees must be widely present between the stars. Different regions of this gas are at somewhat different temperatures, ranging from $3 \times 10^5$ to $3 \times 10^{6°}$ K. This hot gas presumably extends far from the galactic plane, forming a galactic corona, whose presence was postulated in the 1950s as a source of confining pressure for the cool clouds observed far above the plane.

Detailed ultraviolet measures of absorption features, supplementing the much less complete data obtainable from the ground in visible light, have indicated widespread depletion of heavy elements—that is, their abundances relative to hydrogen are often less than the cosmic abundance. This effect, which is most marked for refractory materials of high melting temperature, results from the condensation of elements into the solid particles, or dust grains, known to be present. The depletion is variable, as a result of ongoing processes of grain formation and destruction.

For lines of sight with relatively small amounts of material (low $N(H_{Tot})$), the spread of random atomic velocities found from absorption features of various elements indicates a gas temperature of roughly 8,000° K. This warm gas, revealed also by 21-cm measures, is characteristic of relatively transparent, low-density clouds.

Microwave measurements of many emission features have yielded estimates of relative abundances for dozens of molecules and have also led to determinations of the temperature and overall density of the gas in which these molecules are concentrated. These molecular regions are generally cooler (about 30° K) and denser (some $10^5$ $H_2$ molecules cm$^{-3}$) than the diffuse clouds studied by means of their visible and ultraviolet absorption features. Carbon monoxide produces emission at intermediate densities (exceeding about $10^2$ cm$^{-3}$); such molecules tend to be concentrated in giant clouds some 200 light years across, each with a mass of several hundred thousand times that of the Sun. These clouds contain denser regions, in some of which new stars have recently formed. Formation of bright, massive stars is believed to occur primarily in these giant molecular clouds.

# 7

# A Cloud Model of the Interstellar Gas

In earlier chapters we have discussed recent observations of the interstellar medium and how these are interpreted. The chief findings have been the physical properties of the different regions in the gas— the cold clouds of neutral hydrogen, the regions of warm, ionized hydrogen, and the hot, highly ionized coronal gas, in which even heavy atoms are highly ionized. In the present chapter we shall try to put all this information together, fitting it with a theoretical model.

Model fitting has become increasingly important in recent scientific research. This technique is helpful in bringing together and explaining observations of natural phenomena that are complicated and not under the observer's control. In an effort to fit the observations with theory, a scientist formulates a simplified model, whose behavior and general properties can be computed exactly, and whose characteristics are then adjusted to give the best agreement with the observations. The model will not take into account all the complications of the actual situation. If the scientist is fortunate, the effects considered in the model will turn out to be the ones of primary importance. In such a case, additional observations will generally be consistent with the model, requiring elaborations and refinements but no sweeping changes. Such a model is said to be realistic and gives us new information about Nature. When a model is first presented, its degree of realism is usually not clear, and its tentative acceptance by other scientists often depends not only on its plausibility but also on such aesthetic factors as simplicity, as well as on the general climate of scientific opinion.

For the interstellar medium as a whole, a theoretical model should have two objectives. First, the model should indicate the location of the different regions, presenting a sort of map, or blueprint, of the interstellar gas. If we could travel about the Galaxy, passing through and around clouds, viewing them from all angles, the preparation of such a map would be straightforward. As yet, we cannot escape from the Solar System and must be content with viewing the Galaxy along different lines of sight extending outward from the Earth. Since the shapes and distances of individual clouds are usually known inaccurately, if at all, any such map is necessarily very schematic. A second objective of such a model is to show the changes that occur with time—how the clouds form, evolve, and condense into stars. This latter objective is even more difficult than the former, especially since most of the interstellar gas has shown essentially no change at all during the few centuries in which scientists have recorded what can be seen in the sky.

As a result of these difficulties, this chapter is necessarily speculative. It seems likely that the interstellar cloud models that have been developed during the last few years, which are summarized here, have some elements of truth. But Nature is certainly more complicated than the present simple models. Quite probably, some of the most important processes have not yet been taken into account.

This state of affairs is reasonably typical of the theoretical models that have been developed recently in a wide variety of astronomical fields, with each model designed to fit a wide variety of observational facts. Despite their shortcomings, such models have tremendous value in the development of science. They suggest to both observers and theorists new problems to consider, new questions to ask of Nature. A theoretical model also has the great advantage that it can bring coherence into an otherwise confused picture. In this way a model, even if it is not fully realistic, can help one to remember the individual results of observation and theory.

Before discussing any particular models, we look first at the simplest facts that any model of interstellar clouds must take into account. The discussions in the earlier chapters show that any theoretical model must include the concentration of the cold, neutral gas in relatively dense clouds occupying only a few percent of the volume of the galactic disc. These cold clouds are embedded in warmer gas, much as raisins are embedded in a raisin pudding. This analogy must not be carried too far, however. The cold clouds have an enormous range of masses, ranging from some 30 solar masses for small dark clouds, or globules, up to some $3 \times 10^5$ solar masses for giant molecular clouds. Thus if the smallest clouds correspond to ordinary raisins, each weighing about a sixtieth of an ounce, a giant molecular cloud would correspond in this model pudding to a 10-pound raisin!

Within the last few years we have come to realize that the "pudding" between the raisins is largely a hot coronal gas, at a temperature of roughly a million degrees. The broad extent of this hot gas results directly from the observed rate of supernova explosions, which is about one in every twenty-five years in each galaxy. During $10^6$ years there will be $4 \times 10^4$ supernova explosions in our own Galaxy. Most of these will be in the galactic disc, whose volume, as we have seen in chapter 1, is roughly $10^{13}$ cubic light years. Each supernova remnant will expand violently out to a radius of roughly 300 light years. Hence the $4 \times 10^4$ such explosions occurring during $10^6$ years will sweep out a volume of $4 \times 10^4 \times (4\pi/3)(300)^3$ cubic light years, or about $5 \times 10^{12}$ cubic light years, about half the volume of the galactic disc. Evidently any point in the galactic disc will on the average be swept over by supernova remnants about once every $2 \times 10^6$ years, which is short compared with the $10^7$ to $10^8$ years required for evolution of the cold clouds.

The passage of a supernova remnant through the intercloud medium will tend to sweep away any low-density material present, replacing it with coronal gas. (The swept material will be compressed into a denser, thin sheet by the force of the exploding hot gases and will be cooled to a low temperature, providing additional material for the cold clouds.) Because of this continued sweeping action of supernova remnants, much of the intercloud medium is assumed to be hot coronal gas, an assumption supported by observations of $O^{+5}$ absorption and soft X-ray emission, discussed in the previous chapter.

In the pages immediately following, we shall look at a "snapshot" view of the interstellar gas, summarizing the relationships between the different regions observed. In the subsequent section we shall discuss how the clouds change with time; here the snapshot is replaced by a motion picture, at the cost of an even greater dependence on the imagination of the theorist! Finally, theoretical models are developed to show how new stars are born from clouds.

## STRUCTURE OF CLOUDS

A typical interstellar cloud is more like an onion than a raisin, since it is composed of successive layers, each with its own distinctive properties. The outermost surface layer is affected by the surrounding hot coronal gas. Similarly, the coronal gas is affected by the presence of the cloud. We discuss first how each of these two regions influences the other.

One mutual influence arises because each gas presses on the other. As we have seen in chapter 6, if one gas is at a higher pressure than another, the first will expand, compressing the second, until the two pressures are equalized. For this reason it would seem that the pressure in the intercloud medium must be roughly the same as that in the clouds. Interpretation of the X-ray results indicated a coronal pressure somewhat greater than that obtained for the clouds, but in view of the many uncertainties, this discrepancy is not serious. For calculating physical conditions in the various cloud layers, from the outer, hot coronal gas to the inner, cold core, we shall assume that the pressure is the same in all layers—an example of the kind of simplification made in models.

This assumption of uniform pressure gives useful relationships for the densities and temperatures throughout the successive layers. Since the pressure in a gas is proportional to both $T$, the absolute temperature, and $n$, the number of particles per cubic centimeter (see p. 120), it follows that

$$n(\text{cloud}) \times T(\text{cloud}) = n(\text{intercloud}) \times T(\text{intercloud})$$

where $n(\text{cloud})$ and $n(\text{intercloud})$ denote the values of $n$ in the cloud and intercloud gas, respectively, and similarly for T. Thus,

$$\frac{n(\text{cloud})}{n(\text{intercloud})} = \frac{T(\text{intercloud})}{T(\text{cloud})} \, .$$

From the previous chapter we know that T(intercloud) is about $10^{6\circ}$ K, while discussions in chapters 2 and 5 have shown that in a typical diffuse cloud T(cloud) is about 80° K. Hence the ratio of $n(\text{cloud})$ to $n(\text{intercloud})$ is about $10^6/80$ or 12,500. The value of 40 cm$^{-3}$ found in chapter 5 for $n(\text{H})$ in a typical diffuse cloud gives about $3 \times 10^{-3}$ cm$^{-3}$ for $n$ in the coronal gas; since the hydrogen is virtually all ionized in the coronal gas (in contrast to its predominantly neutral state in the clouds), half of the particles will be free electrons, and the proton density, $n(\text{H}^+)$, will be $n/2$, or about $1.5 \times 10^{-3}$ cm$^{-3}$. In the various cloud layers discussed below, $T$ has intermediate values, and so, consequently, does $n$, with $nT$ again remaining constant.

Another way in which the coronal gas can interact with the cloud material is a result of the large difference in temperature. It is common experience that when a cold body is surrounded by a hot material, heat will flow from the hot substance to the cooler one, a process called heat conduction. This flow of heat tends to cool down the hot material and heat up the cold body. If the temperature of different points is measured accurately, the values will be found to increase smoothly with increasing distance from the center of the cold object.

Exactly this same process must occur at the surface of an interstellar cloud (either cold or warm) surrounded by hot coronal gas. Heat will flow from the surrounding gas into the cooler cloud, cooling down the coronal gas close to the cloud surface. A spherical conductive layer with a reduced temperature forms in the coronal gas surrounding the cloud. The distribution of temperature in such a layer is shown in figure 7.1 for a cross-section of an idealized cloud. Evidently the temperature in the coronal gas decreases gradually some distance from the cloud surface and more and more steeply as the surface is approached. (As we shall see shortly, a cold cloud is surrounded by an envelope of warm gas; the cloud surface shown in figure 7.1 is the outer surface of this envelope.)

The cloud in figure 7.1 is taken to be spherically symmetrical, a convenient, but probably entirely unrealistic, assumption. In figures 1.1 and 1.4, which show expanding material in the Big Bang and the structure of an evolved massive star, respectively, a spherical shape is required by the physical principles involved. In the Big Bang the light waves reaching a point after a travel time $t$ must all have originated on the spherical horizon of radius $c \times t$; for a star it is the strong self-gravitational field that produces a spherical shape. For a cloud, however, there is no strong influence requiring spherical symmetry. Nevertheless, the assumption of such symmetry makes the theory much simpler, and the results obtained should be roughly valid for clouds of more realistic shapes.

The reduced temperatures in the coronal conductive layers around clouds may account for the range of temperatures deduced from the soft X-ray data. Since the fraction of oxygen atoms that have lost five electrons, rather than four, six, or some other number, is strongly peaked at $3 \times 10^{5°}$ K (in a hot gas ionized by collisions with free electrons), the observed $O^{+5}$ absorption lines may originate primarily in these conductive layers, rather than in the hotter, more widely distributed, regions of coronal gas. This point of view is supported by the correlation between the velocity shifts for the $O^{+5}$ absorption features (calculated from the wavelength shifts, assumed to result from the Doppler effect) and the corresponding shifts for the $Si^{++}$ and $N^+$ features, produced in the outer layers of the cloud.

The surface layers of gas in the cold cloud that become heated by thermal conduction from the corona expand and escape from the cloud. Because the heated gas moves away from the cloud surface,

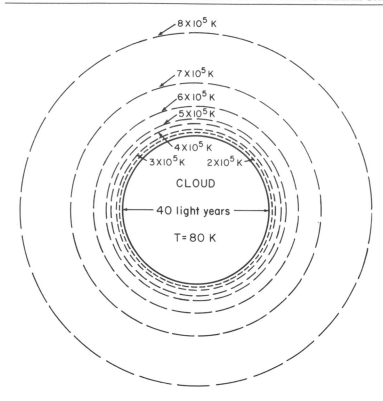

FIGURE 7.1 Conductive layer in coronal gas. The solid circle shows the cross-section of an idealized spherical cloud embedded in a hot coronal gas, whose temperature far from the cloud is taken to be $10^{6°}$ K. Temperatures are indicated on various spherical surfaces (shown by dashed lines) in the conductive layer, which is cooled by the conduction of heat into the diffuse cloud. The diameter of the cloud (including outer layers of warm gas surrounding an inner cold core) is taken to be about 40 light years.

this process is called evaporation, in analogy with the escape of vapor from an evaporating liquid drop. Clouds that are near a supernova explosion and, as a result, become surrounded by gas at temperatures as great as $10^{8°}$ K, may evaporate entirely and disappear. In the more widespread coronal gas, at a temperature of about $10^{6°}$ K, evaporation is significant only for the smaller clouds with a mass less than some 100 solar masses. In fact in some regions, the reverse process, condensation, may occur. Just as water droplets collect as dew on cold grass, so hot gas can condense on cold clouds in certain circumstances.

While heat conduction produces a dominant effect on the structure of the surrounding coronal gas, the structure of the cloud itself is usually influenced primarily by incident photons. These bundles of electromagnetic energy pass freely through the coronal gas but are absorbed in the cloud, where they ionize and heat the gas. Since photons of different wavelengths penetrate different distances into the cloud, a layered structure results. If the cloud is sufficiently massive, the inner region will remain cold. In the model presented here, we take this cold core to be a typical diffuse cloud of the type discussed earlier, with a temperature of 80° K, a column density of $4 \times 10^{20}$ hydrogen atoms $cm^{-3}$, a hydrogen particle density of 40 $cm^{-3}$ and a radius of 7 light years. Figure 7.2 shows such a composite cloud, with the cold, inner core surrounded by two layers of warm gas, an inner and an outer layer, both heated by photons. The cloud and all its inner layers are again shown as spherical, continuing this useful theoretical fiction.

To understand these different layers, we must consider the interaction between the cloud gas and the various photons reaching the cloud. These photons may be divided into three different wavelength groups, each group penetrating successively further into the cloud. These groups are: (a) ultraviolet photons capable of ionizing hydrogen; (b) soft X-ray photons; (c) photons at visible and near-ultraviolet wavelengths.

The photons that are most easily absorbed and that affect the outermost layer of the cloud are those in group (a)—that is, those that have only slightly more energy than is needed to detach an electron from a neutral hydrogen atom. (This energy is 13.6 eV if the atom is in the ground state, the usual interstellar situation.) Such photons have wavelengths in the range from 912 to roughly 500 Å and are produced by hot stars. Many stars of this type are closely surrounded by clouds of dust and gas, which absorb these ultraviolet photons, but some such stars are out in the clear. The photons that they radiate will reach the surfaces even of distant clouds.

Since an ionizing photon of this type is strongly absorbed by neutral hydrogen atoms, it will not get very far into a cloud. On the average, a photon at about 700 Å, for example, will penetrate a hydrogen cloud through a column density of $3 \times 10^{17}$ neutral hydrogen atoms per square centimeter before it is absorbed. Compared with the column density of $4 \times 10^{20}$ $cm^{-2}$ through the inner core, this is a very small amount of material. The gas reached by this ultraviolet ra-

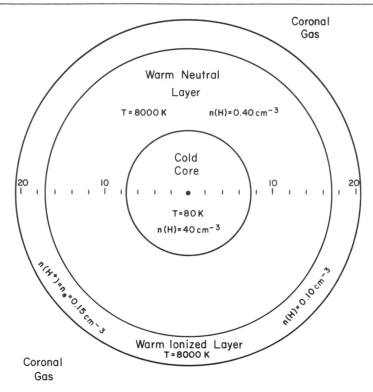

FIGURE 7.2 Structure of a composite cloud. Within the cold, inner core and the two warm, outer layers, the temperature, $T$, and the particle density of neutral hydrogen, $n(H)$, are assumed to have the values indicated. The scale of radii, in light years, is indciated by the numbers along the horizontal scale. The structure of the coronal gas, which surrounds the outer, warm layer, is shown in figure 7.1.

diation will be ionized and heated to about 8,000° K as a result of the photon energies released, forming an ionized, warm layer just inside the cloud surface. Since the pressure in this outer, warm layer must be about the same as that in the cold core, this hundredfold increase in temperature must be offset by a hundredfold decrease in the particle density, $n$. Since many of the hydrogen atoms (about sixty percent) are ionized in this layer, the contribution of $n_e$ and $n(H^+)$ must be included in $n$; as indicated in the figure 7.2, $n_e$ and $n(H^+)$ are equal to 0.15 cm$^{-3}$, with $n(H)$ equal to 0.10 cm$^{-3}$, giving 0.40 cm$^{-3}$ for $n$, one percent of the corresponding value in the cold core.

The values of $3 \times 10^{17}$ cm$^{-2}$ for the column density of neutral hydrogen atoms and 0.10 cm$^{-3}$ for $n(H)$ give a radial thickness of about 3 light years for this warm, ionized layer. This is an appreciable fraction of the 7-light-year radius of the inner, cold, diffuse cloud. About twenty percent of the volume in the galactic disc is occupied by these layers of warm, ionized gas. (Similar warm gas that surrounds hot stars and produces conspicuous emission nebulae such as the Orion nebula discussed earlier, is not included in this estimate.)

Next in order of increasing penetrability are soft X-ray photons, which originate in the hot coronal gas and produce a second layer in the cloud, just inside the shell of warm, ionized gas. These photons have energies mostly in the range from 40 to 120 eV. At 60 eV, which we may take as a typical value, the wavelength is about 200 Å, about a third of that for the ultraviolet photons considered above. These X rays are much less strongly absorbed and on the average will penetrate through a column density of $4 \times 10^{18}$ neutral hydrogen atoms per square centimeter before absorption. (One atom of helium for every ten atoms of hydrogen is assumed; helium contributes about sixty percent of the total absorption of these X rays.) In the gas reached by these energetic photons, a small fraction of the hydrogen atoms, perhaps ten percent, will be ionized. In addition, the ejected electrons will have a large energy of motion and will heat the gas. At least in the outer regions of this layer, the temperature may be as great as 8,000° K. Hence this second, or inner, layer is warm, just like the ionized layer farther out.

Again, physical equilibrium requires that the gas pressure in this inner, warm layer should be the same as in the cold cloud inside and the coronal gas outside. For $T$ equal to 8,000° K in the inner layer and 80° K in the cold core, the density in this second layer is one percent of that in the core, or 0.4 hydrogen atoms per cubic centimeter. (The small contribution of free electrons to the overall particle density is ignored.) The computed column density of $4 \times 10^{18}$ hydrogen atoms per cubic centimeter required for soft X-ray absorption then requires that the computed density within the second layer extend over a radial distance of 10 light years. With a core radius of 7 light years, the outer radius of this inner, warm layer becomes 17 light years. The volume of this layer is thirteen times that of the inner cold core $((17^3 - 7^3)/7^3 = 13)$. The corresponding mass ratio is thirteen percent, when the hundredfold difference in density is taken into account. It is presumably this warm, neutral gas that is seen in 21-cm emission with relatively little absorption and in ultraviolet absorption in unreddened stars. The mass ratio between the warm, neutral hydrogen and the cold hydrogen for this model composite cloud is in general agreement with the observational data, a result that may well be only a lucky coincidence!

Finally we must consider the third category of photons present between the clouds—those of visual and near-ultraviolet wavelengths, radiated by the stars. Most of these photons do not interact with the dominant atoms present, hydrogen and helium, and consequently penetrate very much further into a cloud than do photons of shorter wavelength and higher energy. Most photons with wavelengths longer than 1,000 Å will pass freely through the inner cold core, with its assumed hydrogen atom column density of $4 \times 10^{20}$ cm$^{-2}$. It is these photons that dissociate any $H_2$ molecules that form. In addition, the energetic photoelectrons ejected by grains on absorption of such photons keep the gas temperature from falling below 80° K. As we have already seen, the product $nT$ is the same in this core as in all the surrounding layers, giving the same pressure everywhere.

In some clouds, the column densities through the cold cores will much exceed the average value for diffuse clouds that has been assumed here. With such greater column densities, the character of the gas at the cloud center is altered. Figure 5.2 indicates that for $N(H_{Tot})$ greatly exceeding $4 \times 10^{20}$ cm$^{-2}$, the ultraviolet photons that dissociate $H_2$ become absorbed, and a central region of predominantly molecular $H_2$ forms. For $N(H_{Tot})$ exceeding $10^{21}$ cm$^{-2}$, absorption by dust particles becomes significant, and even visual photons will no longer reach the cloud center. Thus in a typical opaque molecular cloud, the inner core is fully shielded from ultraviolet and visible photons. In such an opaque cloud, the normal heating effects are weak, or absent, and the temperature will fall well below 80° K, reaching 5 to 10° K in the darkest clouds—not far above absolute zero.

Figures 7.1 and 7.2 gave snapshot views of an individual model cloud. To include a variety of clouds in an overall snapshot, figure 7.3 shows a sample region of the galactic plane; each cloud intersecting this plane is represented by its cross-section drawn through the cloud center. Differences between the two types of warm envelopes (ionized and neutral) are ignored in this diagram. As indicated, some small clouds have no cold cores at all. A blast wave produced by the explosion of a supernova is shown advancing through the collection of clouds. The many hundreds of stars within this region are not shown.

The theoretical model summarized in these various figures provides a coherent explanation of a number of different observations and is generally consistent with many of the known physical pro-

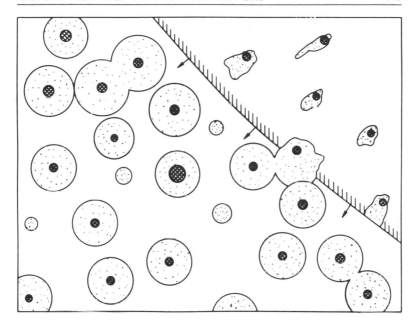

FIGURE 7.3 Snapshot of clouds in galactic disc. Idealized interstellar clouds
are shown, including those that intersect the mid-plane of the Galaxy. The
dark, central cores represent cold, diffuse clouds, with temperatures of about
80° K; the surrounding dotted circles represent warm envelopes, heated to
about 8,000° K. The hot coronal gas fills the space between the clouds. A supernova remnant is expanding into the region from the upper right.

cesses occurring between the stars. However, this model must still be
regarded as a working hypothesis. As a measure of the uncertainties,
the following list indicates a few of the ways in which this cloud
model is somewhat idealized.

1. The spherical form assumed for most clouds and shown in
figures 7.1, 7.2, and 7.3, is certainly not valid.

2. The rates at which ionizing ultraviolet photons and soft
X-ray photons stream on to a cloud are not known accurately and
may be inadequate to maintain these layers at the assumed temperatures; other physical processes may therefore be involved. In
addition, these rates are likely to be quite different at different lo-
cations in the galactic disc.

3. The variations in temperature, density, and fractional ion-

ization throughout each layer have not been considered. It is likely that the temperature diminishes with increasing depth and increasing photon absorption. This effect will lead to an increase in particle density (to maintain constant pressure) and a decrease in thickness (to maintain constant N(H)), since the absorption through the layer must be roughly fixed).

4. The warm envelopes outside the central, cold cloud will tend to be swept away by passing supernova remnants and may then drift about as separate clouds without cold cores. During the short times between successive passages of supernova remnants (about $10^6$ years) the cold clouds will generally not have time to fully re-form their surrounding warm envelopes. Such problems of cloud evolution are relevant to the pages immediately following.

Evidently the details of shapes, dimensions, and structures of clouds shown in figure 7.3 are uncertain. However, the general picture of somewhat separate, cold clouds, surrounded by warm layers and moving about through the much hotter coronal gas is probably close to reality.

## CLOUD EVOLUTION

We now inquire what happens when the cloud model snapshot in figure 7.3 becomes one frame in a motion picture, with successive frames showing conditions about four hundred years apart. If the picture is shown at a normal projection rate of 24 frames per second, one second of such a film will show changes over about 10,000 years. A million years will be spanned in a projection time of about two minutes. An hour will cover about $3 \times 10^7$ years, less than one percent of the age of the universe, but comparable with the lifetime of an individual cloud.

Even at this vastly accelerated projection rate, the changes will still appear leisurely. A typical diffuse cloud, with a speed of about 10 km sec$^{-1}$, will take about one minute to move a distance equal to its diameter (about 14 light years, not including the warm envelope). Every few minutes an explosive blast wave from a supernova will appear, sweeping across the screen. The clouds and their envelopes will be in a constant state of flux. Mutual collisions between two clouds will lead sometimes to coalescence into a single cloud, sometimes to formation of several fragments moving independently. Shreds of envelopes torn off clouds by collisions or passing supernova remnants will drift hither and you, sometimes evaporating into the hot gas, sometimes coagulating with other such fragments or passing clouds.

Occasionally a giant molecular cloud, perhaps extending over as much as two hundred light years, will drift by. In some such clouds star formation will be going on, and around newly formed stars a hot gas of ionized hydrogen will be expanding, compressing the colder material around it into new clouds.

Such a film will show tremendous activity, with constant changes on all sides, with clouds forming, growing, colliding, evaporating, and condensing into stars. However, the general overall appearance of this melee will be much the same at the end of our one-hour film as it was at the beginning. About the same number of clouds will be present, moving at the same average speeds and undergoing the same types of cataclysms.

In a biological system, populations usually tend to remain relatively steady, while individuals are born, grow, become subject to experiences of all types, and die. The same is true of clouds in interstellar space. The system of interstellar clouds remains nearly steady, although a single cloud is in constant flux.

What can a scientist do to analyze and clarify this chaotic, but stationary, state of affairs? How can a theory be developed to give numbers that can be compared with observations? In principle, there are two steps in such an analysis. The first step is to catalog each process—each reaction that can alter the cloud population—and to compute the rate at which it occurs. For interstellar clouds, such a computation requires specific numbers for the rates at which clouds of different sizes collide with other clouds—that is, the number of such collisions that will occur during each million years in some large volume, say a cube a hundred light years on a side. The scientist must also have numbers for the fraction of such collisions that lead to the coalescence of two clouds into a larger cloud and the fraction that lead instead to fragmentation of one or both clouds. In view of the complicated nature of cloud-cloud collisions, we cannot compute these numbers exactly, but estimates of statistical probabilities are possible.

The second step is to put together the information on these different processes and to determine the average properties of the cloud population that results. In particular, how many clouds of different sizes and masses will be present in the varying, but statistically steady, conditions that we have watched in the motion picture? If the characteristics of the expected cloud distribution are computed, a comparison of theory with observation will be possible. If the two sets of numbers are in general agreement, it is likely that the theory has taken the most important processes into account.

In this section, some tentative first steps in this direction will be described. As an example of the way in which astronomers try to fit the real world with idealized models, a very simplified model of cloud evolution, based on five simple, if unrealistic, assumptions, is presented. After the consequences of this model have been explored, we shall then examine the changes expected if these assumptions are modified to be more realistic.

The model is based on the following assumptions:

1. Clouds of small mass (at most 100 solar masses) are formed from expanding gas around a hot star or supernova—see assumption 5.

2. The clouds grow by coalescence; every two clouds that collide with each other will stick together to form a cloud of greater mass. (Since the warm envelopes discussed above contain only a small fraction of the total mass, they are ignored here.)

3. The number of collisions occurring between clouds with identical masses is proportional to the square of the number of such clouds present but is unaffected by differences in the shape, size, or speed of the clouds. (Quantitatively, let $n_j$ be the number of clouds of some type $j$ in a standard volume of $10^6$ cubic light years. Since each single cloud collides more often the greater the number, $n_j$, of other such clouds around it, the total number of collisions among all such clouds in this same volume, during a standard time of $10^6$ years, equals $Kn_j^2$. The constant $K$ is assumed independent of $j$—that is, $K$ is the same for clouds of all types.)

4. Collisions between clouds of different masses are ignored.

5. When a cloud exceeds a certain critical mass, perhaps about $3 \times 10^5$ times that of the Sun, the cloud collapses because of the gravitational force of the matter on itself. A small fraction of the cloud condenses into stars, whereas all other material is expelled by the expanding gas around these newly formed stars or around supernovae that form subsequently. It is this ejected material that forms new clouds of small mass—see assumption 1.

According to this model, the interstellar clouds have their own cycle, being born with low masses and then coalescing to form more and more massive clouds. Finally, the very biggest clouds collapse to form some new stars, with most of the gas returning to the interstellar medium and starting the cycle afresh.

We now combine these assumptions to determine for this simple model the relative number of clouds present with different masses. In accordance with assumption 4 above, the only collisions considered are those between clouds of the same mass. If all newly born clouds have initial masses equal to $m_1$, coalescence between them will produce clouds of mass $2m_1$. Collisions between clouds of mass $2m_1$ will then produce clouds of mass $4m_1$, and so on to $8m_1$, $16m_1$, $32m_1$, etc. In a standard volume, which we again take to be that of a cube of dimension 100 light years, there will be many clouds with each of these masses. We denote by $n_1$ the number of clouds present with the lowest mass, $m_1$; similarly $n_2$, $n_4$, etc. represent the corresponding numbers for clouds of mass $2m_1$, $4m_1$, etc. (For a cloud with a mass $m_j = jm_1$, the number of such clouds present in the standard volume of $10^6$ cubic light years is denoted by $n_j$.)

In a steady state the number of clouds of a particular mass formed in a standard time (again taken to be $10^6$ years) must just equal the number of clouds of that same mass that disappear by coalescence. If this were not so, clouds of a particular mass would either accumulate or gradually disappear, contrary to the steady-state assumption. To obtain specific results, we apply this steady-state condition to clouds of some particular mass, which we take to be $8m_1$.

The rates of cloud formation and disappearance may be evaluated on the basis of assumption 3 above. A cloud of mass $8m_1$ is formed when two clouds of mass $4m_1$ collide. The number of such collisions is proportional to $n_4^2$. Clouds of mass $8m_1$ disappear when two such clouds coalesce to form a cloud of mass $16m_1$. The number of such collisions is proportional to $n_8^2$. However, every collision between two clouds of mass $8m_1$ leads to the disappearance of both clouds, while each collision between two clouds of mass $4m_1$ forms only one cloud of mass $8m_1$. Hence the steady-state condition for clouds of mass $8m_1$ tells us that $n_4^2$ must be twice as great as $n_8^2$.

(Quantitatively, the number of $8m_1$-mass clouds forming in the standard volume during the standard time equals $Kn_4^2$, while the corresponding number of such clouds disappearing is $2Kn_8^2$; equating these two gives $n_4^2 = 2n_8^2$, or $n_8/n_4 = 1/\sqrt{2}$. Since $n_4/n_2 = n_2/n_1 = 1/\sqrt{2}$ also, multiplying these three ratios together shows that $n_8/n_1 = 1/\sqrt{8}$; more generally, $n_j/n_1 = 1/j^{1/2} = [m_1/m_j]^{1/2}$.)

This result can be clarified by an analogy with music. Two tones are an octave apart if the frequency, $\nu$, of one is twice the frequency of the other; an octave may sometimes refer to all tones with frequencies between some value $\nu$ and $2\nu$. Similarly, we can define an octave of mass values as the range of masses between some mass $m_j$ and twice this value. Thus $n_1$, $n_2$, $n_4$, etc. are the numbers of clouds in successive mass octaves. The preceding paragraph has indicated that an increase in $m_j$ by one octave (that is, by a factor of 2) decreases $n_j$ by $1/\sqrt{2}$. Hence $n_j$ varies as $1/\sqrt{m_j}$. (The total mass of clouds that have a specific mass, $m_j$, equals the product of $m_j$ and $n_j$, which varies as $\sqrt{m_j}$, increasing as the square root of the mass.)

Now that the consequences of this model have been worked out, it is natural to ask how the predicted distribution of clouds changes when various improvements are made in the model. Assumption 4, that clouds collide only with others of identical mass, is clearly unrealistic. If this assumption is changed to permit coalescence of two clouds with different masses (but the assumption that collision rates are unaffected by differences in cloud shape, size, or speed is preserved), the argument becomes more involved. However, the same result as before follows; $n_j$ again varies inversely as the square root of the cloud mass, $m_j$ (provided that $m_j$ appreciably exceeds the mass at birth and is appreciably less than the mass at which gravitational collapse begins). This is reasonable, since in this more general case the coalescence of clouds with comparable masses is still the dominant process. For a cloud of appreciable mass, collisions with clouds of much lower mass are much the most numerous, but their overall effect is relatively small because of the small masses involved. Collisions with clouds of much greater mass can also be ignored, since the number of more massive clouds is relatively very small, and the rate of these collisions is therefore substantially less than the rate at which a cloud collides with others of about its own mass.

What is more surprising is that the results are not greatly altered when assumption 3 above is further relaxed by taking into account the dependence of collision rate on cloud size and velocity. To some extent these effects cancel out, since a cloud of relatively high mass has a large area, which tends to make collisions with other clouds more frequent, but also a low velocity, which tends to reduce the collision frequency. The chief advantage of assumption 3 is that it gives very simply the exact result that $n(m)$, the number of clouds in a mass octave centered at $m$, varies $1/\sqrt{m}$.

The neglect of other collisional processes, in accordance with assumption 2, is more serious. It is certain that for some types of collisions fragmentation, rather than coalescence, is the primary end result. For example, when two clouds are involved in a grazing collision, only a small amount of material at the edges of the two clouds will be subject to mutual physical impact. The rest of the material will be relatively unaffected; interstellar clouds have no more internal strength, or rigidity, than clouds of water vapor in the Earth's atmosphere. Most of the material in the two clouds will continue to move along separate paths as though nothing had happened, leaving behind one or more fragments of material that collided.

Some attempts have been made to analyze fragmentation collisions theoretically and to include their effects in the cloud evolution model. Other effects that have been included are evaporation of cloud material through the conductive layer into the coronal gas, the sweeping away of warm envelopes by passing supernova remnants, increases in cloud mass above the minimum value required for gravitational instability, and growth of a cloud by accretion of material from supernova shells. Although these further theoretical studies are somwhat tentative, their result is generally to decrease the theoretical relative number of low-mass clouds and to increase the fraction of the interstellar medium found in the somewhat more massive clouds. The coalescence model already showed a slow increase with $m$ of the total mass in clouds per octave of mass $m$. This tendency appears strengthened by the somewhat more exact computations. The general trend of these theories is in accord with the large amount of material observed in the giant molecular clouds.

Assumptions 1 and 5 form the basis of the general cycle of cloud formation: growth, condensation, disruption, and rebirth. Like the other assumptions, they are not correct in detail. Under some conditions stars can probably form from clouds much less massive than the giant molecular clouds. Moreover, the most massive clouds may form directly by condensation of gas in a very large region of the Galaxy, rather than by collisions and coalescence. It is also possible that other effects, such as infall of fresh gas into the Galaxy from intergalactic space, may be of great importance in cloud evolution. In future research, the cloud evolution models discussed here will doubtless be modified and expanded to include such additional phenomena.

## FORMATION OF STAR GROUPS

The greatest challenge to any model of the interstellar gas is to explain how clouds condense to form new stars. Before examining the theoretical models developed for star formation, we review the observational results that such models must explain. As pointed out in chapter 2, we know that the very luminous young stars (whose nuclear fuel can support their high rate of energy output for at most a few million years) are concentrated in the arms of spiral galaxies, supporting the view that these stars are formed from the gas and dust that is also concentrated in such arms. A closer study of where these young stars are found gives further information on the environment required for star formation.

Young stars are generally located in groups. Evidently, gas between the stars condenses to form aggregations of new stars, either stable clusters bound together by mutual gravitational attraction or transient associations, expanding as the stars move away from each other at speeds of a few kilometers per second. The tendency of young stars to form these expanding associations was first shown systematically by the Soviet astronomer V. A. Ambarzumian in 1947. Clearly, a major task of star formation theory is to show how groups of new stars are born together.

An important characteristic of such groups is that their age can be determined. After a group has formed, the most massive stars, which burn their nuclear fuel most rapidly, will be the first to run out of energy and die (producing supernovae in many cases). The next brightest stars will die later, and so on. The brightest remaining stars are about to die next and must be nearing the end of their fuel supply; hence their age can be calculated.

When this analysis of age is applied to specific groups of young stars, an important result on the location of star formation is found. In a number of cases, several adjacent groups of stars are found on a line across the sky, with the oldest group at one end and the youngest at the other. Recent measures of carbon monoxide emission show that in such situations the youngest group tends to border a giant molecular cloud, which suggests that this cloud has been the birthplace of the successive stellar groups.

Such observational evidence, obtained from star groups and molecular clouds in Orion, is shown in figure 7.4. The solid lines show the outlines of the carbon monoxide–emitting regions. One of the two regions (the southern, or lower, one in the figure) is among the closest giant molecular clouds. The distance of this cloud is about 1,500 light years, and its length about 200 light years. The dashed curves indicate the approximate boundaries of different groups of young stars, with the age of each group indicated. (These four groups constitute what is called the Orion I association of young stars.) The youngest stellar group, designated Id in the figure, is at the center of the luminous Orion nebula.

These data strongly suggest that star formation in this area started some twelve million years ago at a boundary of a molecular cloud, which was then more extensive than it is now, and has gradually eaten its way into the cloud, leaving behind a succession of star

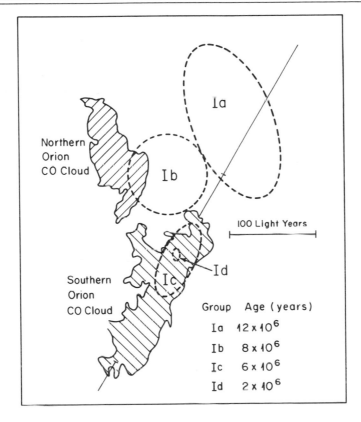

FIGURE 7.4 Molecular clouds and groups of young stars in Orion. The solid-line contours enclose two giant molecular clouds, distinguished by diagonal hatching. The four dashed-line contours enclose groups of young stars, with the ages indicated. Group Id is centered in the Orion nebula. All four stellar groups are about 1,500 light years from the Sun. The straight line from lower left to upper right is parallel to the galactic plane. (Along this line the galactic latitude, $b$, = $-19.4°$, while the galactic longitude, $l$, ranges from 200 to 215°.)

groups, whose ages increase with distance from the present region of active star formation. Around the older stellar groups there is now relatively little gas. Any material left over from star formation has presumably been blown away, either by the outward-moving warm gas, ionized and heated by newly born, hot stars, or by the supernova remnants produced by the subsequent explosion of dying stars.

A variety of observations give results similar to those found in

Orion. Regions of recent star formation can be detected either from the presence of hot, newly born stars or from the brightly radiating, ionized hydrogen gas that surrounds them. Even if obscuring dust hides the visible light from these regions, radio emission betrays the presence of warm, ionized hydrogen. Infrared emission is also observed from the heated dust particles surrounding these obscured young stars. Sky maps show that a number of such star-forming regions are located at the apparent boundaries of conspicuous, giant molecular clouds. In other cases a star-forming region may well be located at a cloud boundary but is actually seen from the Earth in projection against a cloud—that is, as seen from the Earth, the region is either right in front of or right behind the cloud. Because of all this evidence we assume that at least the more massive stars are formed at the boundaries of giant molecular clouds.

Next we consider how theoretical models might fit these observations. In particular, we look at a recently developed model that is based on a triggering mechanism, by means of which the birth of one star in a molecular cloud triggers the formation of one group of stars, which triggers the formation of the next group and so on—a little like knocking down a line of dominoes.

This theory is based on the processes occurring when a massive new star is born. Such a star produces vast amounts of radiation, including many ultraviolet photons. These photons will ionize the hydrogen and heat the gas, just as they do in the warm envelope surrounding a cold cloud as discussed earlier in this chapter. The increase in temperature produces a corresponding increase in pressure, and the hot ionized gas literally explodes, pushing the cold, neutral gas radially outward and compressing it so that its pressure increases to match the pressure of the driving ionized gas.

It turns out that these two changes in the cold gas—compression and acceleration on the one hand, ionization of hydrogen atoms and gas heating on the other—occur in two relatively thin layers, each of which is called a *front*. The surrounding cold gas of neutral atoms is first compressed and accelerated outward in a *shock front*. Then it becomes ionized (and also heated) in a subsequent *ionization front*. The shock front moves outward into undisturbed gas at a speed of some 3 km sec$^{-1}$, much greater than the speed of sound, which is about 0.3 km sec$^{-1}$ in the cold gas. Such shock fronts are usually produced by objects moving faster than the speed of sound such as supersonic airplanes or rifle bullets. For the conditions relevant here (shock-front velocity ten times the velocity of sound and temperature held constant by radiation), the gas density is increased about a hundredfold by compression in the shock front.

The ionization front also moves outward, trailing closely behind the shock front. Since neutral hydrogen gas absorbs strongly the energetic ultraviolet photons from the newly born, hot stars, any such photons reaching the ionization front will not penetrate much further. As a result, the hydrogen gas ahead of this ionization front is almost entirely neutral; behind this front, most hydrogen atoms have lost their electrons and become ionized.

The two outward-moving fronts are depicted in figure 7.5. The layer of cold, compressed neutral gas between these two fronts is the site of star formation, according to this model. The thickness, d, of this layer is very small, at most 0.1 or 0.2 light years (some $10^{12}$km), which is perhaps about one percent of the lateral extent of the layer. For clarity of presentation a much thicker layer is shown in the figure.

The compressed layer will start to condense into stars when the self-gravitational attraction of the gas produces a collapse into many fragments. As we saw in chapter 1, the condition for gravitational collapse of an initially uniform gas was computed by Jeans, who

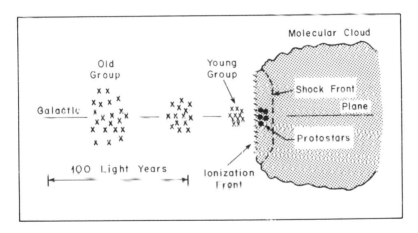

FIGURE 7.5 Model of star formation in a molecular cloud. The young group of stars at the right, next to the giant molecular cloud, has been formed within the last two million years. The pressure of the hot, ionized gas around these stars pushes on the cloud, generating a shock front, which advances into the cloud. Behind this shock front there follows an ionization front, in which neutral hydrogen atoms are ionized by ultraviolet light from the stars. Between these two fronts is a cold, compressed layer (actually much thinner than shown) that is collapsing gravitationally, forming several hundred protostars.

found that collapse would occur for any mass greater than a critical value, which is now called the Jeans mass. (Quantitatively, this Jeans mass, $M_J$, is given by $M_J = C^3(\pi/G)^{3/2} \rho^{-1/2}$, where C is the speed of sound in the isothermal gas, $\rho$ is the gas density, and G is the gravitational constant.) To apply this result to the present situation, we may think of the compressed layer as divided into individual cubes, each of width d and volume $d^3$. As more and more gas accumulates in the cold, compressed layer, the mass in each of these cubes will increase. When the mass in a cube exceeds the Jeans mass, one would expect the cube to collapse, forming a dense, prestellar cloud, or *protostar*. If the layer is a hundred times as wide as it is thick, the number of such cubes, and hence of protostars, will be $10^2 \times 10^2$, or $10^4$.

The model used by Jeans in his computations assumed a uniform gas, extending in all directions. For the cold layer between two fronts, it is more realistic to adopt a slab model, with a finite thickness. Calculations for such a model show that gravitational collapse starts with lateral motions parallel to the plane of the layer and only later involves compression perpendicular to the plane. The most unstable gaseous blobs, which are those most likely to form protostars, turn out not to be cubes but are rather shaped like squat pill boxes, with an average width parallel to the layer equal to four times the layer thickness. Hence the total number of such blobs, or pill boxes, in the entire layer, if the width is 100 d, is 25 × 25, or about 600. Computations also show that the minimum mass of each blob required for gravitational collapse is about one-fourth of the Jeans mass. It is not surprising that the results obtained with this more realistic model should differ appreciably from those found with the simplified model of Jeans.

These model calculations may be applied to the situation expected in the cold layer between the two fronts. All the collapsing masses will be assumed to be identical, each taken to be a blob of the most unstable size. Although in fact a wide distribution of sizes and masses is expected, computations for a group of identical protostars should give a reasonable picture of the average properties to be expected.

In this picture, all the blobs will start to collapse when their masses exceed the same critical value, equal to 3 solar masses. This value is based on a temperature of 20° K, a plausible value for an opaque molecular cloud. (The corresponding speed of sound C, is about 0.3 km sec$^{-1}$.) It is possible that the newly formed stars may heat the dust and gas in their neighborhoods; if a temperature of 100° K is assumed for the neutral hydrogen gas, this critical mass rises to about 35 solar masses. The particle density within the layer is taken to be $10^5$ hydrogen atoms $cm^{-3}$, a hundredfold increase over the typical density of $10^3$ hydrogen atoms $cm^{-3}$ in a molecular cloud. (One helium atom for every ten hydrogen atoms is assumed.) This compression factor is what one would expect from a shock front moving outward at a speed of 3 km $sec^{-1}$. If the lateral extent of the star-forming layer is taken to be about 10 light years, as indicated by the observations, the total mass of the cold layer that starts to collapse is a few thousand solar masses. In theory only a fraction—perhaps ten percent—of the mass in these various protostars actually condenses into stars; in fact, a mass of a few hundred Suns is frequently found in a young stellar group. Thus the computed mass in the young group agrees roughly with the observations.

To summarize this model of protostar formation, the ionization and shock fronts produced by newly born, hot stars near the edge of a molecular cloud move together into the cloud. Material continues to accumulate in the cold, compressed layer between these two fronts, of thickness d, until the mass of gas in a volume $16d^3$ exceeds the critical value for gravitational collapse. At this point, the gas within the layer starts to condense into hundreds of separate protostars, many of which contract further to form a group of stars. The two fronts continue their outward motion, maintained in part by ultraviolet radiation from these youngest, hot stars. However, the layer between the two fronts now contains relatively little mass and must travel an appreciable distance before it contains enough material to condense gravitationally into another several hundred stars. The distance observed between different groups of new stars is about equal to that obtained from the theory.

Although this model has had a number of successes in explaining the observed data, it does encounter several difficulties. For instance, why does the gas wait until the arrival of the shock front before condensing gravitationally? As we have seen, the Jeans mass $M_J$ varies inversely as the square root of the density. Hence, if the Jeans mass in the layer is 13 solar masses, then before the hundredfold compression in the shock front, $M_J$ should already be some 100 solar masses. The total mass of gas in the cloud is actually much greater than this. Why doesn't it condense? This difficulty is a general one in any discussion of giant molecular clouds, many of which are known to be gravitationally unstable according to the usual simplified analysis. We are reasonably sure that in general these clouds are not collapsing. The worry of the theorist at this point is that whatever process is holding up the clouds against their own self-attraction may also be operating in the compressed layer between the two fronts, thereby preventing the type of star formation discussed here. Until the internal motions and dynamical equilibrium of giant molecular clouds are better understood, we cannot get much of a handle on this intriguing problem, although several suggestions have been made. Despite this and other problems, the process described here has attractive features and is about the only one for which a detailed theoretical model has been presented.

Alternative processes for protostar formation may also be possible. For example, compression of a molecular cloud by a supernova remnant produced by dying stars of one generation could lead to the birth of the next stellar generation. This process has not yet been analyzed in much detail.

## FROM PROTOSTAR TO STAR

The theoretical scenario described above follows a giant molecular cloud through the process of condensation into many separate prestellar objects or protostars. Protostars are somewhat denser than the compressed layer from which they form but are still enormously more extended and rarefied than the stars into which they presumably condense. How do protostars shrink from a good fraction of a light year in size down to a typical stellar diameter—a few million kilometers, or about $10^{-7}$ light years? This phase of star formation is difficult to follow observationally, since the obscuring clouds of dust form a cosmic womb, or shell, which most light waves cannot penetrate. Hence the models of this process are mostly deductive and cannot be compared readily with any detailed observations. A few of these models are described here. As we shall see, some features of these models are drastically altered when the underlying assumptions are made somewhat more realistic.

The simplest model is the collapse of a sphere of cold gas, assumed to start from a motionless state with the same density everywhere. Because of the low temperature, pressure forces are negligible, and all elements of the sphere are accelerated inward by their mutual gravitational acceleration. It is easy to demonstrate mathematically that the inward gravitational acceleration and the resulting inward velocity are both linearly proportional to the distance from the center, and hence that all elements of the sphere take the same amount of time to reach the center. Of course the model is no longer applicable when all the gas has piled up in the central region. Before this pileup the density is the same everywhere in the collapsing sphere at any one time. One important result given by this model is a specific value of the time required for the complete collapse of a cold cloud, amounting to about $10^5$ years if the initial density is $10^5$ hydrogen atoms $cm^{-3}$.

A more realistic model takes into account the temperature of the gas and the resultant internal pressure. For simplicity, the calculations assume that the temperature is constant and that the collapse is spherical, starting from a motionless state. The pressure forces are most important near the outer regions of the sphere; since the external pressure is low, the internal pressure in the outer layers does not increase as rapidly as in the inner layers. The resultant difference in pressure produces an outward force. Hence the outer layers do not collapse to the center as rapidly as the inner layers. After the inner layers have collapsed, the outer ones reach the center at progressively later and later times. Qualitatively this is an entirely different picture from that obtained with the cold sphere of uniform density. In this more realistic picture, large differences in density appear, and after a while the density varies with the radial distance, $R$, approximately as $1/R^2$.

An even more detailed analysis shows that the inner regions will form a heated core, and that a shock front will develop when the outer layers start to pile on to this core. In one version of this model, the inner regions form a bright, hot star, whose ultraviolet radiation ionizes and heats the outer layers, pushing them away before they have reached the central regions. In this way the process limits to about 50 solar masses the amount of material that can condense, perhaps explaining why no stars are observed with masses much higher than about this value.

The assumption of spherical symmetry, with all velocities directed either toward or away from the center, is obviously not very realistic. In particular this assumption excludes the possibility that the cloud could condense into more than one star. (The possibility of fragmentation into many stars was discussed in the first chapter). More realistic models must follow the evolution of a cloud in three dimensions, taking into account motions in all three directions. The necessary computations could, in principle, be carried out with a sufficiently powerful computer.

The chief problem with such a three-dimensional model is that computers with the necessary power do not yet exist. The difficulty is that when a gas is flowing, some rather small-scale effects usually appear—either small eddies or small condensations, which in interstellar clouds are likely to be present initially in any case. To handle such effects accurately requires a very large grid of points. In a particular volume, at least a hundred points along each dimension are needed to obtain adequate resolution, and a thousand points would be better. Hence in this entire volume, $10^6$ points are a minimum, with $10^9$ points desirable. Such physical quantities as the velocity, density, and temperature must be evaluated at each point for each of many hundred time-steps. In a few years computers sufficiently powerful to handle such problems may be available. If so, they will be useful for analyzing not only the evolution of interstellar clouds but also the motions in the Earth's atmosphere that control the weather.

With the computers currently available some preliminary three-dimensional models of cloud collapse have been constructed with a grid of only about 18,000 points. These computations show that an initially spherical cloud that collapses gravitationally undergoes little fragmentation. Because of low spatial resolution this result is not conclusive but raises some doubt as to the conditions under which fragmentation occurs.

There are several other problems that future models of star-forming clouds must take into account. For instance, what about the effects of magnetic fields produced by electric currents in the ionized interstellar gas? Such fields are known to be present. Although the laws governing these fields are clear, our understanding of the ways in which such fields affect interstellar phenomena is not clear at all. Yet these magnetic effects may be of predominant importance in certain aspects of star formation. In addition, cloud rotation cannot be ignored. Such rotation probably plays a particularly important part in the formation of double stars and planetary systems.

Our knowledge of how stars form from interstellar gas is rough, uncertain, and tentative. Although much has been learned, and some exciting results have been obtained, most of the joy of discovery is still ahead.

## SUMMARY

Supernova remnants go flying past any point in the galactic disc every $2 \times 10^6$ years on the average, sweeping away any low-density gas between the cold clouds. This process guarantees that much of interstellar space will be occupied by the hot ($10^{6°}$ K) coronal gas within these remnants.

Between a cold cloud and the surrounding hot, coronal material, several different layers are formed. Heating by soft X-rays produces a warm ($10^{4°}$ K) envelope of neutral hydrogen atoms surrounding the cold cloud. Outside this, ultraviolet photons form a thinner, warm envelope, in which much of the hydrogen is ionized. The conductive flow of heat from the hot coronal gas into the outer envelope of the cloud cools the hot gas somewhat and produces some evaporation from the cloud envelope.

According to preliminary models of cloud evolution, the clouds are formed from expanding gas around supernovae or hot stars and are destroyed by collisions among clouds. The cloud population, however, remains constant, containing clouds of widely different masses. These theoretical models indicate that the galactic disc as a whole contains somewhat more interstellar material in the relatively scarce, larger, more massive clouds than in the more numerous, smaller, less massive ones.

Observations suggest that young, massive stars are born in groups at the edges of giant molecular clouds. Star formation from the material in these clouds is thought to occur when the gas is compressed by an interstellar explosion produced by an earlier generation of hot stars. A tentative theoretical model has been developed, attributing this explosion to rapid expansion of hydrogen gas, ionized and heated by the ultraviolet light from this earlier stellar generation. The outward-rushing gas compresses the cold material in front into a thin layer, which then collapses under its self-gravitational attraction, forming separate prestellar condensations, or protostars. The number of protostars formed at one time and their total mass, as predicted by this model, appear roughly consistent with observations.

Simplified models have also been presented for the contraction of an extended protostar to form a new star (powered by nuclear fusion). Although this process is difficult to observe directly and may be too complex to follow in detail with existing theoretical techniques, the models serve to indicate the roles that various physical processes can play in this cosmic drama.

# Bibliography

## READINGS AND REFERENCES

For each chapter of this book, the following text refers to a variety of relevant publications and indicates the subjects discussed in each one. The general reader may be interested in some of the nontechnical and semipopular books listed in the first of the two bibliographies; these writings provide some added information on interstellar studies, particularly those discussed in the first three chapters of this book. In the second bibliography scientists will find references to the specific technical papers underlying this book; these may be helpful in identifying the astronomers involved and will serve as a guide to the more detailed research results.

### Chapter 1. The Cosmic Cycle of Birth and Death

An excellent nontechnical summary of the Big Bang has been given by Weinberg (1977), which has served as the primary source of information for the first section. The material in the two subsequent sections—on galaxy formation and element generation in stars—has been taken from the thorough technical review articles by Gott (1977) and Trimble (1975), respectively. A popular account of the cosmic cycle has been given by Field, Verschuur, and Ponnamperuma (1978, chapters 2 and 3). For references to supernova remnants and star formation, see chapters 2 and 7, respectively, below.

### Chapter 2. The Interstellar Medium as Viewed in 1970

This topic is covered in a number of popular books on astronomy. Good basic discussions of matter and radiation (and also on the electromagnetic spectrum, treated in chapter 3) appear in texts by

**163**

Jastrow and Thompson (1977, chapters 2 and 4) and Wyatt (1977, chapter 11). Observations of the 21-cm hydrogen feature and of visible absorption features, together with the properties derived for the interstellar medium, are discussed by Wyatt (1977, chapters 18 and 21) and also by Abell (1977). A very thorough discussion of interstellar matter and supernova remnants appears in the "serious popular" book by Shklovskii (1978, chapters 2, 3, and 16).

For technical reviews of interstellar matter studies as of about 1970, with references to other works, see Kerr (1968) for 21-cm research, Münch (1968) for research on visible absorption features, and Greenberg (1968) for studies of dust grains. Brief technical monographs dealing with these and other interstellar topics have been written by Spitzer (1968, 1978); the latter reviews work in 1971–72 on the determination of gas temperature from comparison of absorption and emission at 21 cm. Outstanding observational results on interstellar sodium absorption features observed with a very narrow measurement band are reported by Hobbs (1969).

Emission from ionized gas at a temperature of some $10^{4°}$ K, in both visible light and radio waves, has been discussed extensively in a technical book by Osterbrock (1974). The status of soft X-ray research at the beginning of the 1970s is reviewed in a technical summary by Silk (1973). The discussion of supernova remnants is based on a thorough technical review by Gorenstein and Tucker (1976) and on the theory summarized by Spitzer (1978). Recent data on the composition of fast-moving clouds in the Cassiopeia supernova remnant have been taken from Chevalier and Kirshner (1978). The section on supernova remnants makes some use of observational data obtained throughout the 1970s. In broad outline these later data do not differ qualitatively from those obtained during the 1960s (for comparison, see the review by L. Woltjer, 1972) but are generally much more precise.

### Chapter 3. New Windows on the Universe

A readable, nontechnical discussion of ultraviolet space astronomy in general and the *Copernicus* program in particular has been given by Goldsmith (1974). The Skylab program is clearly described in a well illustrated book by Lundquist (1979). As regards technical papers, the reader is referred to Rogerson, Spitzer, and co-workers (1973) for a detailed description of the telescope-spectrometer on *Copernicus* (including its performance in orbit) and to Penzias and Burrus (1973) for a discussion of microwave detectors capable of operating at the 0.26-cm wavelength of the carbon monoxide emission feature. The principles of superheterodyne receivers are described in many texts on radio techniques (see Timbie 1973). The results obtained from the Skylab soft X-ray detector are described by Vanderhill and colleagues (1975), while Margon, Mason, and Sanford (1974) report the related results obtained for several bright stars with the Copernicus X-ray instrument.

### Chapter 4. Primordial Hydrogen in the Galactic Disc

A technical review of ultraviolet space astronomy, covering the topics in chapters 4, 5, and 6, has been given by Spitzer and Jenkins (1975). The monograph by Spitzer (1978) covers this same material from a more theoretical point of view, as part of a general discussion of interstellar matter research. Systematic results on hydrogen column densities have been obtained by Bohlin, Savage, and Drake (1978). Research on the deuterium-hydrogen ratio, based on the original paper by Rogerson and York (1973), has been summarized by Laurent, Vidal-Madjar and York (1979), whose results have been used here.

### Chapter 5. Clouds of Molecular Hydrogen

A technical survey of the $H_2$ spectrum and its application in interstellar matter research was given in 1966 by Field, Somerville, and Dressler. Systematic data on strong interstellar $H_2$ absorption features have been reported by Savage and co-workers (1977) and have been analyzed recently by Federman, Glassgold, and Kwan (1979), following principles first outlined by Solomon and subsequently utilized in the pioneering analysis by Hollenbach, Werner, and Salpeter (1971); these researchers compute the fraction of hydrogen atoms bound in $H_2$ molecules and, as a result, the column density $N(H_2)$, which determines the absorption of ultraviolet radiation passing through an interstellar cloud. The use of $H_2$ absorption features for determining the temperature within dense clouds is largely based on the work by Savage and colleagues (1977), whereas the values of the overall hydrogen density, $n(H_{Tot})$, and the photon absorption time have been taken from Jura (1975), who made use of observational data by Spitzer, Cochran, and Hirshfeld (1974). The direct measurements of cloud diameters have been carried out by Knude (1980). For a general discussion of interstellar chemical processes involving molecular hydrogen, see the review by Watson (1978). Detailed theoretical computations of molecular abundances under interstellar conditions have been reported by Mitchell, Ginsburg, and Kuntz (1978).

**Chapter 6. Heavy Elements between the Stars**
The basic observations on interstellar clouds at large distances from the galactic plane (high z) were published by Münch and Zirin (1961). A theoretical analysis of these data, which indicated the presence of a galactic corona, was carried out by Spitzer (1956). Cox and Smith (1974) analyzed the generation of such a pervasive hot gas by supernova remnants. A detailed analysis of $O^{+5}$ absorption features observed by *Copernicus* has been published by Jenkins (1978), whereas Burstein and colleagues (1977) have presented and discussed data on soft X-rays observed with a sounding rocket. A lower limit for the coronal temperature was obtained by York (1974). The nature of the corona implied by all these observations has been discussed by Chevalier and Oegerle (1979).

The composition of the interstellar gas, as found from ground-based data and the *Copernicus* observations, was extensively analyzed for the line of sight toward Zeta Ophiuchi by Morton (1975); he utilized the theoretical discussion by Field (1974) to investigate how the relative abundance of each element depends on its condensation temperature. Recent information on this dependence has been given by Snow, Weiler, and Oegerle (1979). Systematic surveys of interstellar features in some sixty stars have been made by Stokes (1978) for titanium and by Savage and Bohlin (1979) for iron. The absorption features in the unreddened star Alpha Virginis have been measured and analyzed by York and Kinahan (1979), who determined the gas temperature from the spread of atomic velocities for various elements. The processes involved in the growth and destruction of grains have been considered by Draine and Salpeter (1979).

The properties of molecular clouds have been summarized in technical reviews by Zuckerman and Palmer (1974) and Thaddeus (1977). The giant structures seen in carbon monoxide were discussed at a conference on this topic; see especially the broad survey by Solomon and Sanders (1980) in the conference proceedings.

**Chapter 7. A Cloud Model of the Interstellar Gas**
The properties of individual clouds as presented here are mostly

based on the pioneering technical paper by McKee and Ostriker (1977). The nature of the conductive interface with the coronal gas has been analyzed by Cowie and McKee (1977). The observed correlation of velocities indicated by $O^{+5}$, $Si^{++}$, and $N^+$ absorption features has been presented by Cowie and co-workers (1979). The interaction between clouds and supernova remnants is also discussed by Cox (1979), whose alternative model differs in several respects from that summarized here. The discussion of cloud evolution begins with the coagulation model first presented by Field and Saslaw (1965); the physical explanation given here for their results is new. The effects of fragmentation are taken into account in papers by Cowie (1980) and by Chièze and Lazareff (1980).

Observational evidence on groups, or associations, of young stars has been summarized by Blaauw (1964). The extensive, more recent observational results relevant to star formation have been summarized in a technical review by Kerr (1977) and in other papers published in the same conference proceedings. The sequential formation of stellar groups, resulting from the steady expansion of warm, ionized gas into a giant molecular cloud, has been analyzed in some detail by Elmegreen and Lada (1977) and by Elmegreen and Elmegreen (1978). Further detailed discussions of this process have been given by Lada (1980) and by others at a conference on molecular clouds (see references for chapter 6). Larson (1973, 1977) has summarized theoretical work on later stages in the star-formation process. Three-dimensional calculations on the gravitational collapse of protostars have been presented by Tohline (1980). A general brief summary of star-formation theories has been given by Woodward (1978).

## NONTECHNICAL BOOKS

Abell, G. 1975. *Exploration of the Universe*. 3rd ed. N.Y.: Holt, Rinehart and Winston.

Field, G. B., Verschuur, G. L., and Ponnamperuma, C. 1978. *Cosmic Evolution*. Boston: Houghton Mifflin.

Goldsmith, D. 1974. Chapter 23 in *Heritage of Copernicus*, ed. J. Neyman, National Academy of Science. Cambridge, MA: MIT Press, pp. 487–507.

Jastrow, R., and Thompson, M. H. 1977. *Astronomy: Fundamentals & Frontiers*. 3rd ed. N.Y.: Wiley.

Lundquist, C. A., ed. 1979. *Skylab's Astronomy and Space Sciences*. NASA.

Shklovskii, I. S. 1978. *Stars, Their Birth, Life and Death*. Translated from the 1975 Russian text by R. B. Rodman. San Francisco: W. H. Freeman.

Weinberg, S. 1977. *The First Three Minutes*. N.Y.: Basic Books.

Wyatt, S. 1977. *Principles of Astronomy*. 3rd ed. Boston: Allyn & Bacon.

## TECHNICAL BOOKS AND PAPERS

Blaauw, A. 1964. *Annual Review of Astronomy and Astrophysics* 2: 213.

Bohlin, R. C., Savage, B. D., and Drake, J. F. 1978. *Astrophysical Journal* 224: 132.

Burstein, P., Borken, R. J., Kraushaar, W. L., and Sanders, W. T. 1977. *Astrophysical Journal* 213: 405.

Chevalier, R. A., and Kirshner, R. P. 1978. *Astrophysical Journal* 219: 931.

Chevalier, R. A., and Oegerle, W. R. 1979. *Astrophysical Journal* 227: 398.

Chièze, J. P., and Lazareff, B. 1980. *Astronomy and Astrophysics* 91: 290.

Cowie, L. L. 1980. *Astrophysical Journal* 236: 868.

Cowie, L. L., Jenkins, E. B., Songaila, A., and York, D. G. 1979. *Astrophysical Journal* 232: 467.

Cowie, L. L., and McKee, C. F. 1977. *Astrophysical Journal* 211: 135.

Cox, D. P. 1979. *Astrophysical Journal* 234: 863.

Cox, D. P., and Smith, B. W. 1974. *Astrophysical Journal* (Letters) 189: L105.

Dickey, J. M., Salpeter, E. E., and Terzian, Y. 1978. *Astrophysical Journal Supplements* 36: 77.

Draine, B. T., and Salpeter, E. E. 1979. *Astrophysical Journal* 231: 438.

Elmegreen, B. G., and Elmegreen, D. M. 1978. *Astrophysical Journal* 220: 1051.

Elmegreen, B. G., and Lada, C. J. 1977. *Astrophysical Journal* 214: 725.

Federman, S. R., Glassgold, A. E., and Kwan, J. 1979. *Astrophysical Journal* 227: 466.

Field, G. B. 1974. *Astrophysical Journal* 187: 453.

Field, G. B., and Saslaw, W. C. 1965. *Astrophysical Journal* 142: 568.

Field, G. B., Somerville, W. B., and Dressler, K. 1966. *Annual Review of Astronomy and Astrophysics* 4: 207.

Gorenstein, P., and Tucker, W. H. 1976. *Annual Review of Astronomy and Astrophysics* 14: 373.

Gott, J. R. 1977. *Annual Review of Astronomy and Astrophysics* 15: 235.

Greenberg, J. M. 1968. *Stars and Stellar Systems*, vol. 7, pp. 221–265. Chicago: University of Chicago Press.

Hobbs, L. M. 1969. *Astrophysical Journal* 157: 135.

Hollenbach, D. J., Werner, M. W., and Salpeter, E. E. 1971. *Astrophysical Journal* 163: 165.

Jenkins, E. B. 1978. *Astrophysical Journal* 220: 107.

Jura, M. 1975. *Astrophysical Journal* 197: 575, 581.

Kerr, F. J. 1968. *Stars and Stellar Systems*, vol. 7, p. 575. Chicago: University of Chicago Press.

Kerr, F. J. 1977. *Star Formation*, ed. T. de Jong and A. Maeder, p. 3. IAU Symposium No. 75. Dordrecht: Reidel.

Kerr, F. J., and Westerhout, G. 1965. *Stars and Stellar Systems*, vol. 5, p. 178. Chicago: University of Chicago Press.

Knude, J. 1980. *Astronomy and Astrophysics Supplements* 38: 407.

Kutner, M. L., Tucker, K. D., Chin, G., and Thaddeus, P. 1977. *Astrophysical Journal* 215: 521.

Lada, C. S. 1980. *Giant Molecular Clouds in the Galaxy*, ed. P. M. Solomon and M. G. Edmunds, p. 239. New York: Pergamon Press.

Larson, R. B. 1973. *Annual Review of Astronomy and Astrophysics* 11: 219.

Larson, R. B. 1977. *Star Formation*, ed. T. de Jong and A. Maeder, p. 249. IAU Symposium No. 75. Dordrecht: Reidel.

Laurent, C., Vidal-Madjar, A., and York, D. G. 1979. *Astrophysical Journal* 229: 923.

Margon, B., Mason, K. O., and Sanford, P. W. 1974. *Astrophysical Journal* (Letters) 194: L75.

McKee, C. F., and Ostriker, J. P. 1977. *Astrophysical Journal* 218: 148.

Mitchell, G. F., Ginsburg, J. L., and Kuntz, P. J. 1978. *Astrophysical Journal Supplements* 38: 39.

Morton, D. C. 1975. *Astrophysical Journal* 197: 85.

Münch, G. 1968. *Stars and Stellar Systems*, vol. 7, p. 365. Chicago: University of Chicago Press.

Münch, G., and Zirin, H. 1961. *Astrophysical Journal* 133: 11.

Osterbrock, D. E. 1974. *Astrophysics of Gaseous Nebulae*. San Francisco: Freeman.

Penzias, A. A., and Burrus, C. A. 1973. *Annual Review of Astronomy and Astrophysics* 11: 51.

Rogerson, J. B., Spitzer, L., Drake, J. F., Dressler, K., Jenkins, E. B., Morton, D. C., and York, D. G. 1973. *Astrophysical Journal* (Letters) 181: L97.

Rogerson, J. B., and York, D. G. 1973. *Astrophysical Journal* (Letters) 186: L95.

Savage, B. D., and Bohlin, R. C. 1979. *Astrophysical Journal* 229: 136.

Savage, B. D., Bohlin, R. C., Drake, J. F., and Budich, W. 1977. *Astrophysical Journal* 216: 291.

Savage, B. D., and Mathis, J. S. 1979. *Annual Review of Astronomy and Astrophysics* 17: 73.

Silk, J. 1973. *Annual Review of Astronomy and Astrophysics* 11: 269.

Snow, T. P., Weiler, E. J., and Oegerle, W. R. 1979. *Astrophysical Journal* 234: 506.

Solomon, P. M., and Sanders, R. A. 1980. *Giant Molecular Clouds in the Galaxy*, ed. P. M. Solomon and M. G. Edmunds, p. 41. New York: Pergamon Press.

Spitzer, L. 1956. *Astrophysical Journal* 124: 20.

Spitzer, L. 1968. *Diffuse Matter in Space*. New York: Wiley.

Spitzer, L. 1978. *Physical Processes in the Interstellar Medium*. New York: Wiley.

Spitzer, L., Cochran, W. D., and Hirshfeld, A. 1974. *Astrophysical Journal Supplements* 28: 373.

Spitzer, L., and Jenkins, E. B. 1975. *Annual Review of Astronomy and Astrophysics* 13: 133.

Stark, A. A., and Blitz, L. 1978. *Astrophysical Journal* (Letters) 225: L15.

Stokes, G. M. 1978. *Astrophysical Journal Supplements* 36: 115.

Thaddeus, P. 1977. *Star Formation*, ed. T. de Jong and A. Maeder, p. 37. IAU Symposium No. 75. Dordrecht: Reidel.

Timbie, W. H. 1963. *Essentials of Electricity*, 3d ed., revised by A. L. Pike. New York: Wiley.

Tohline, J. E. 1980. *Astrophysical Journal* 235: 866.

Trimble, V. 1975. *Reviews of Modern Physics* 47: 877.

Vanderhill, M. J., Borken, R. J., Bunner, A. N., Burstein, P. H., and Kraushaar, W. L. 1975. *Astrophysical Journal* (Letters) 197: L19.

Vidal-Madjar, A., Laurent, C., Bonnet, R. M., and York, D. G. 1977. *Astrophysical Journal* 211: 91.

Watson, W. D. 1978. *Annual Review of Astronomy and Astrophysics* 16: 585.

Woltjer, L. 1972. *Annual Review of Astronomy and Astrophysics* 10: 129.

Woodward, P. R. 1978. *Annual Review of Astronomy and Astrophysics* 16: 555.

York, D. G. 1974. *Astrophysical Journal (Letters)* 193: L127.

York, D. G., and Kinahan, B. F. 1979. *Astrophysical Journal* 228: 127.

York, D. G., and Rogerson, J. B. 1976. *Astrophysical Journal* 203: 378.

Zuckerman, B., and Palmer, P. 1974. *Annual Review of Astronomy and Astrophysics* 12: 279.

# Index

**173**

# Silliman Volumes in Print